simple things

JIM BRICKMAN

with
CINDY PEARLMAN

Hay House, Inc.
Carlsbad, California • Sydney, Australia

Published and distributed in the United States by:
Hay House, Inc., P.O. Box 5100, Carlsbad, CA 92018-5100
(800) 654-5126 • (800) 650-5115 (fax)

Editorial supervision: Jill Kramer
Cover Design: Christy Salinas
Interior Design: Jenny Richards

Cataloging-in-Publication Data

Brickman, Jim.
    Simple things / Jim Brickman with Cindy Pearlman.
        p. c.m. -- (Hay House lifestyles)
    ISBN 1-56170-923-9 (hardcover)
        1. Simplicity. I. Pearlman, Cindy, 1964- II. Title. III.
    Series.

BJ1496 .B75 2001
179'.9--dc21   2001039351

ISBN: 1-56170-923-9

04 03 02 01   4 3 2 1
1st printing, September 2001

Printed in the United States of America

contents

simple things

It used to be so simple. We came home from school and did the things that most kids do: We ate three Twinkies, drank milk right out of the carton (although under torture or DNA testing we'd never admit to it), and then sat down in front of the television to warp our minds. And we loved it.

We led simple lives—no fax machines, e-mails, or cell phones. Even more remarkable, there was no such thing as a two-way pager! Growing up in Cleveland, the way a kid was paged to dinner was quite basic: "Turn that music off and come downstairs— now!" Mothers would bellow it so loudly that it was a wonder that half a dozen neighborhood kids (and some stray animals) didn't also show up.

We even ate simple foods—disgustingly simple at times. Meat in loaves. Liver with onions. Chicken followed by the word *surprise*—you didn't want to ask. Just shake and bake, baby. It was easy.

We didn't have MTV, VH1, MSNBC, CNN, or high-speed cable Internet access. We had bikes and driveways, and brothers and sisters to torment. There were no super-fast XZT Razor Gliders that cost $99.99—we flew down the driveway even faster in that "borrowed" shopping cart from the local market. Back then, everything was easy to comprehend. Glue wasn't prefaced with the word *crazy*. It was Elmer's. Our friends were the kids across the street . . . not six people making $600,000 an episode named Rachel, Ross, Monica, Joey, Phoebe, and Chandler.

Our lives were pretty good. So what happened that made it so much more complex?

That was the question that a friend and I were asking the other night. Of course, we were on our cell phones, calling each other from airports, after we checked our e-mail and "E" tickets on this "E ride" that our lives have become.

My job touring the country with my music had me on the way to Vancouver, 30,000 feet in the air. My friend, who works for various newspapers, was stuck at a place worse than hell—Los Angeles International Airport—where she was waiting for the red-eye. We missed dogs (hers), houses (mine), and our own comforters (beige and purple, respectively)—it was old friends talking on the phone, moaning about life. "We've just got to simplify things," I said. It was a modest longing, but an important one.

That's the basis of this book: *Simple*

Things. It's about our generation of baby boomers, who among other things, need to slow things down, because yes, we've been listening to that Eagles song. And Don Henley warned us that life in the fast lane would make us . . . well, *exhausted* and *numb* come to mind.

You want a second opinion? Just ask actress Catherine Zeta-Jones, who laughs when she says, "I drive a Range Rover with a cell phone. If you need me, page, beep, fax, or e-mail me. And even if you do all of the above, I might not return your call." Of course she can't call you back—she's too busy.

I began to wonder what made me qualified to write about this topic, besides the fact that my new album is called *Simple Things* and I've been pondering the topic for a couple of years . . . and counting. But let me start with a disclaimer: I don't have a

Ph.D. after my name; I'm not a shrink—yes, I took a psychology class in college, but only as a way to avoid having to struggle through taking calculus. I think I got a *B*.

But I do have certain qualifications to write this book that I humbly want you to consider. For instance, I've always been driven. If I decide I want to do something, I figure out a way to get it done. If I want to meet someone, I do. If I want to travel somewhere, I usually end up getting there. I'm a hard worker, a good son, and an enthusiastic uncle. I can even make pretty good French toast—even if I do set the smoke detectors off. The local fire department doesn't seem to mind a few false alarms.

And last but certainly not least: When friends ask for advice, I have a really good ear, and I do my best to tell them the truth. They call often; they call in the middle of the night. Maybe that's the reason for this book—I need some sleep.

Of course, friends of mine will tell you that it's a good thing I'm not writing a home fix-it book. I can barely even work my own dishwasher, let alone come to terms with anything that includes the dreaded words "some assembly required."

And while we're on the topic, I'll tell you a few more of my faults. I lose my keys on a daily basis—three times last year, the grocery store had to call me to pick them up. But I'm hoping you won't hold that against me. Also, I can't tell you what the latest fashion trends are, unless it involves sweatpants and T-shirts. Did I mention that I also lose my sunglasses—the good ones—regularly? At which point, you might be thinking, *Yeah, Jim, my Ray-Bans are gone, too.* But I'm worse—have you ever lost the new pair the day you've bought them? *I'm totally absentminded.*

As I mentioned, I'm not mechanically inclined. I can't work the VCR or the stereo—which is bad when you're in the music business. My clocks all have different times. I'm really impatient. I don't even sit really well. I have a hard time sitting in a room watching TV or reading. I feel like I've always got to be stimulated.

And that's also why I'm writing this book. Baby boomers feel like they've always got to be stimulated, which is why our lives are governed by our mechanics. We live our lives playacting to our video cameras. We exist by ignoring people, because before saying hello to any member of your family, it's required in modern life to check the answering machine, click on the computer and glance at the e-mail, and then waltz over to the VCR to make sure it's set up—because God only knows, you can't watch *The West Wing* while *The Sopranos* is on—although you don't really have time to watch either of them—it's important that you at least have them on tape.

Stop.

Take a breath.

It's over. A new life is just beginning.

I'm like you. I'm sick of living on a treadmill where life is just about work and money—never stopping to enjoy what you're running so hard for in the first place. The cliché that no one ever said on their deathbed, "Gosh, I wish I'd spent more time at the office," is true.

I want simple things, and you want simple things. Even Madonna wants simple things, which I know sounds odd, but it's true. The other day, she was talking about her dreams, and none involved a cone bra. She said, "I would give anything to just sit in a park with my children on a brilliant spring day and talk to the other mothers."

Sandra Bullock, who just lost her beloved mother, Helga, to cancer, says, "I would give anything to have my mother run her hand through my hair one more time and just say, 'Everything will be all right.'" And Neve Campbell insists, "When I'm feeling stressed, I only want one thing: I want to go home and put on my fuzzy blue slippers. If my house was on fire, they're what I would save first."

Simple things. We want to be able to appreciate a beautiful day. We long for that pulse-pounding joy of looking across a room and seeing our friends. We want to capture some of that childlike wonder where the world is a mystery, and every time we step out the door, there's an adventure just waiting around the corner.

Who knows? At the end of this book, maybe I won't even care if I can't read directions, because the real directions that help you lead a happier life are easy to remember. They're basic.

And speaking of basics, I'll confess to one of the real reasons this book exists—my hair. Stick with me a minute. The other morning I'm looking in the mirror. I'm sort of bleary-eyed, and in my fog, I see this gray hair sticking out. I'm suddenly zapped into full consciousness. I'm also full of questions, such as *When did my hair begin to betray me? Is this a curse? Why me?* Come on—your first gray hair is a big deal, because it's like aliens have invaded. Meanwhile, I'm staring at this hair in horror, thinking, *What is this? And of all the hairs, why does the gray one have to stick out?*

Those are the moments that hit you like a brick. And while I stood in my bathroom, I realized that no one was going to snip off that gray hair for me—I needed to do it myself. If only I could find what I did with the damn scissors, which are probably with my keys and my sunglasses.

It's the same thing with your life: You have to do it yourself. Why would you think that anyone should tell you how to live your life or what choices should be made? You're on your own. The bottom line is that *you* are the only person who can hit the pause button on your life. Your boss can't do it; your wife or husband can't do it. You are the sole owner of your own personal control panel. And at any time, you can stop and reevaluate, rewind and reconsider, or hit *play,* but it's time to get back in a very different sort of game. This time, the win isn't about money, fame, or prestige. It's about your saving your heart and soul in a world that doesn't put much value on either anymore.

Think about it for a minute: Your entire life is defined by your accomplishments—a bachelor's degree, a vice presidency, or

$10 billion in record sales. But what's *really* of value might be a completely different sort of résumé that you'll never write. Good parent. Good friend. Good person. Warm laugh. Good listener.

Good things . . . simple things.

SIMPLE THOUGHT:

*"So here we go.
Let's just dance. Teach my
soul to take this chance."*

— Jim Brickman, from the song "Simple Things"

first things first

Could you do me a favor before we start? Kill your cell phone. Okay, don't hurt the thing, but just temporarily lose it. Then turn off your computer. I know "you've got mail"—so does the rest of the world, but it can wait. Oh, and one more thing: Don't answer the five phones in your house. You've already talked to your mother three times yesterday, and nothing much is really new.

Here's one of the simplest things of all: Just do one thing. Just read. In silence. Just think. Without interruption.

Hey, I know it feels strange. After all,

we've been taught to multitask—I can talk on the phone while typing on my keyboard and having a conversation with someone in my office while the TV is blaring in the background and I'm putting on my jogging shoes. I ask you: Is this a good thing? Should I win an award for it? Is there an Olympic event called "Doing Ten Things at Once"? And most important: Do I focus on anything anymore? Or are my thoughts so jumbled and does my mind race at such a speed that there's no putting on the brakes?

Take a breath. Relax. Inhale. Exhale. Hey, I know it feels strange.

But now we're ready to begin.

SIMPLE THOUGHT:

"Our life is frittered away by detail. . . . Simplify, simplify."

— Henry David Thoreau

quick things

I know that other books suggest that you can wake up one morning and—*whammo!*—change your life. If only things were *that* simple. Instead, may I suggest just giving yourself one medium jolt? Why not make a conscious choice to change *one thing* in your daily routine?

Here are 15 rather painless ways to give your life a tiny shove and change it for the better.

1. Vow for one 24-hour period not to check your e-mail.

2. Remove one appliance from your kitchen counter that you never use. Who has the patience to make homemade lasagna noodles unless Julia Child is coming to visit? Throw out *Presto, It's Pasta!*, instead of letting it remain under six inches of dust.

3. Add one living thing to your home, whether it be a plant or a pet. Both will give you a reason to smile.

4. Make a list of ten things you want to accomplish in the next month—*not* in the next year. Who keeps those promises? How many times have you said, "I vow to lose ten pounds by December. I know! I'll start on November 30th, at midnight. Thank goodness it's only March now." A

month makes it less easy to forget to put off a goal. Now make a separate list of everything you've done in your life that someone once told you was impossible.

5. Wake up 15 minutes earlier in the morning. Use that time for yourself, whether it be writing in a journal, meditating, or lounging in a bath-tub. If you feel guilty about it, just remember that Oprah does all of the above on a daily basis, and no one ever dared call her lazy.

6. Close your eyes and think of your most ridiculous nagging fear. Make a conscious decision not to worry about it anymore.

7. Clean out that one drawer in your kitchen that probably wouldn't pass inspection if the Board of Health were to drop by. You're right in thinking that no home needs 500 loose rubber bands, 90 paper clips, or that jar of gooey stuff that not even the cast of *The X-Files* could identify.

8. Try eating while doing nothing else—not reading or watching TV.

9. Think about the dumbest show you watch on TV on a regular basis. Now take that time and spend it with your child, spouse, or a friend—with the tube turned off.

10. Lie down in the grass in your backyard and look up at the sky. Stay

there for at least ten minutes, unless you're under some kind of horrible bug attack.

11. Call an adult version of a "snow day"—even if it's 80 degrees and sunny outside. And since this is your personal day, make it about *yourself.*

12. Decide once and for all that if a relationship in your life is causing you nothing but a world of pain, walk away in the least harmful and hurtful way possible.

13. Say *no* at least three times in one day. Marvel at how you didn't suddenly turn into the most horrible person on the planet, second only to The Grinch.

14. Find a porch or a playground swing. I don't care how old you are, or if you think it's silly, or if you're worried about breaking the thing. Start swinging.

15. Don't talk. Just listen for once. *Really listen.*

SIMPLE THOUGHT:

*"Slow down.
We all move way too fast."*
— Jim Brickman

c h i l d h o o d   t h i n g s

We've come this far, and I believe I forgot something important.

Let me introduce myself: I'm Jim Brickman, and I play the piano. What other big stuff do you need to know? Since we're on the large matters, let me tell you that I grew up in Shaker Heights, Ohio, where I was the fat kid. And I mean large, but not in charge. Gym class was the horror of my early life, as I was the last kid ever picked for any sports, and under protest, too—I would hear, "I guess we're stuck with *him*." Consequently, I would pray for doctors' notes. "Please excuse Jim from basketball.

He has a hangnail that may require surgery someday."

I also had a very active imagination. I was always coming up with excuses that weren't true to get out of school activities. "Jim can't attend school today because his mother is in labor." I didn't mean she was having a baby. She was working that day at the local library—*in labor*—and couldn't drive me.

Both of my parents came from the same eight-block suburban neighborhood in Cleveland and went to the same high school and college. They were the classic '50s love story—inseparable even when my dad was in the army. They got married before he enlisted, and Mom went with him to several places that had "Ft." in the address. As expected, they came home, got married, and settled into a life of suburbia and red shag carpeting.

It's funny what comes to you when you think about your childhood: Spaghetti-O's in a can; *The Munsters* on TV; my parents' divorce when I was ten.

Sorry, we're about to hit a few rough patches.

After the divorce, it was just me, my mom, and my brother . . . and I was in my own little world. I was the oldest, the "grown-up boy." Very responsible. My brother, Michael, on the other hand, was the popular kid. He was smart and went with the flow. He might tell you that I tried to beat him up from time to time. I guess I was jealous that he had friends and was picked for the teams. But enough with my issues.

My parents' divorce actually brought us together like The Three Musketeers. And now I sit here and marvel at how tough it was on my mother to be a single parent in the '70s. She worked all day as a librarian, and then rushed home to make dinner for us kids. At night, she still had the energy to check if anyone was bleeding or if we were doing our homework. And magically, the bruises were kept to a minimum, as my brother and I became closer as we got older. At night in our bunk beds, we'd make plans for the future. We were comrades in pajamas, sharing a common goal: There in the darkness, we would talk about keeping the three of us close as a family.

The music was always there, too. But I'm not going to tell you some story of a childhood genius who sat down at a piano at age two and started playing like Mozart. My first piano teacher told my mother that I sucked. She said, "Basically, Mrs. Brickman, Jim doesn't have any talent, and it's a waste of money for you to continue these lessons." But you don't mess with Sally Brickman's boy. Oh, no! Mom snapped back, "I don't care if he's any good at it! He likes doing it, and if it makes him happy to play the piano, what difference does it make if he's not a virtuoso?"

Her words—simple, direct, and powerful—stick with me even now, because I'm still not intensely competitive. And I'm grateful not to be that way. I feel like my mom taught me that what makes you happy inside counts, not what other people think of you.

Let me tell you about my first real public performance. Imagine a recital of geeks like myself inside a stuffy gym. I was stuck in the middle of the program, which gave me enough time to sweat in my ruffled dress shirt that encased my stomach bulge.

I wondered, *Did Beethoven ever feel like he was having a fat day from too many wild boar sandwiches? Did he, like me, eat nacho-cheese Doritos? And would he allow all those protruding ruffles from his shirt to affect his performance?* Probably not. At that recital, I gave them my best nonspectacular song—people politely applauded and then raced home to catch the last half hour of *Laugh-In*.

Okay, now let's speed this up. I found a home playing piano at the local community playhouse, The Heights Youth Theater, where I met my best friend, Wendy Leonard. Her father owned the place, and Wendy and I communed with other artistic types.

As a lark, I entered a Cleveland best-band contest with my other good friend, Anne Cochran. We recorded the song "We're All Alone," and one day I got a call that our band had won. We even became locally famous, to the point that the Holiday Inn in Erie, Pennsylvania, wanted to book us for a week.

Anne looked at me like I'd gone nuts.

She reminded me, "We don't have a band. We don't have an act. And we're 15 and can't drive." I hate it when Anne's right. Anyway, I honestly didn't think my mom would call the school and say, "Could you excuse James—he has a gig in Scranton?" But in my heart, I was ready . . . to be 35. Even if no one else wanted me to grow up that fast.

Fast forward to Case Western Reserve University in Cleveland, where I started what became an extremely successful jingle business—kitty litter, toilet bowl cleaner, soda pop, laundry detergent, you name it. This meant I actually had some dough for the first time in my life. But I always wanted to cut a record, which is why in 1988, I moved to Los Angeles, stared with horror at the *Baywatch* bodies lounging by my apartment complex's swimming pool, and began writing music. Three homesick years later, I got a recording contract.

I knew I'd finally made it the day I went into Tower Records and my music wasn't lumped into the miscellaneous "B's"—I had my own plastic separator that said "Jim Brickman." And it hit me: The simplicity of solo piano music found a home in people's hearts. All I had to do was play a piano and that's what connected with people. It was amazingly simple.

As for my music, it includes songs such as "Valentine" and "The Gift." There are also collaborations with singers Carly Simon, Kenny Loggins, Olivia Newton-John, Martina McBride, and Donny Osmond. Maybe you don't know all the words, because I hear that many people make out to my albums, which strikes me as funny. Imagine—the fat kid who didn't have a lot of friends and who couldn't get a date is now responsible for nationwide nookie!

Inside, there are days when that shy boy still lurks, and he reminds me that it's good to look back to your roots and see how you started out. You didn't get from A to Z without a few pit stops in between. And maybe you haven't looked back for a long time— it's tedious, time-consuming, and can even be painful.

But unlike most of the roads out there, Memory Lane is never really closed. And I suggest a short mental road trip from time to time as a life "checkup." I know when I travel down there, I see a few things that make me smile: my mother, my brother, and all that shag carpeting.

SIMPLE THOUGHT:

"Call your mom and dad or brother and sister. Jot them a note. You might even consider actually putting a stamp on the note and mailing it. But seriously, these people had a starring role in the first chapters of your life, and it's time to write them back in for another act."
— Jim Brickman

appreciate things

The other morning, I decided to take a walk around my home, which is up in the canyons of Los Angeles. It's weird that I travel the globe but often don't walk outside my door to look around my own neighborhood. But that's typical of my generation of wanderers who always think something better is somewhere else, when often the best thing of all is right in front of you.

At dawn in Los Angeles, the sky is milky white with big marshmallow clouds forming over the mountains. On a spring morning, the air is so crisp and clean that it almost tickles when you take a deep breath.

Five steps from my front yard, a silver coyote with big eyes stops. My heart leaps, but I'm not breakfast for him—just a curiosity. It suddenly reminds me that no matter where you live, adventure is lurking.

The coyote beats a quick retreat into some shrubs and . . . now, you won't believe this part, but I swear it's true: George Clooney comes walking by me. We stop and talk for a moment; it dawns on both of us that we actually live in the same neighborhood. I get the feeling that he's also been a bit too busy to look around.

I walk higher up into the canyon, where the smell of greenery is better than any $200 bottle of perfume bought at Bloomingdale's. Two deer are off in the distance—they stop, and so do I—and at once I realize that life is miraculous and all around me. The simplest thing of all is to just open your eyes and appreciate it.

We don't just close our eyes at night; we live in a time where our eyes are closed most of the time. For instance, when is the last time you stopped to marvel that your hands are the same shape as your mother's? Or observed that the turbulent clouds before a summer thunderstorm are truly magnificent? Or noticed that a beautiful piece of classical music on your car radio makes your heart feel like it's expanding to the point where it might burst—but not in the same way it felt after eating that meatloaf at the local greasy spoon.

You won't be able to appreciate these things forever. I'm at an age where friends are beginning to lose parents. And anyone who's ever sat among cancer patients in a hospital knows that they long for healthy moments like these: They want to savor a hot summer night, drive with all the windows open, or experience the carefree feeling of watching children play in a backyard.

We've all found ourselves complaining that life stinks, or isn't fair—and maybe that's true, but there are degrees of unfairness. When you're lying on an examining table being told that you only have a few weeks to live, *that* is unfair—no doubt about it, it's the ultimate form of unfair.

When my friend Olivia Newton-John was told she had breast cancer, it wasn't fair; in fact, it was awful. So when you're stuck picking up the kids, going to the grocery store, and cooking dinner in a span of two seconds, it's really not that bad.

And face it—our lives *aren't* that bad. Our grandparents are the ones who came here from other countries. They didn't speak English and were forced to take any type of job just to put food on the table. Multiple families lived in tiny apartments, struggling to get through each and every day just to make life better for their children.

Yes, we might work more hours. The world is more competitive; it's rough out there. But many of us have lovely homes with two-car garages, three television sets, and enough food to survive a short-lived atomic attack. But we're still not happy. We think life is lacking because we don't have the *bigger* house and the *better* car and a lifestyle that might cause Robin Leach to stop by and want to interview us for *Lifestyles of the Rich and Shameless*.

It's just not Shangri-La—no wonder we don't open our eyes. We're too busy looking inside, feeling so sorry for ourselves. Bottom line: Life is actually pretty great, especially if you reduce it down to the small moments.

SIMPLE THOUGHT:

"The happiest of people don't necessarily have the best of everything. They just make the most of everything that comes their way."

— Unknown

favorite things

What gives me the greatest joy? Oh my God, is that a sickening question or what? There are days when I don't feel like being a joyful person. And I hate people who say, "Happiness is when what you say, what you do, and what you think are in harmony."

Sure, it sounds good. Man, it even sounds deep. But what the hell does this mean? Even a shrink couldn't figure it out—although it might look good on a Hallmark card.

My joy is measured in calories. Brownies will do. I can tell you right now that I don't have a favorite vegetable . . .

well, maybe carrot cake. Some people might use illegal substances to get high, but a hot-fudge sundae from Dairy Queen will do it for me. And I know I'm supposed to say that world peace would make me sleep better at night—and frankly I'm all for it—but I also sleep pretty well when my baseball team, the Cleveland Indians, wins. I should also tell you that the best advice I ever got didn't come from my mother—even though she most assuredly saved me from certain death as a kid by forbidding me to swim within 20 minutes of eating a potato chip. My best advice came from Carly Simon, who scolded me for being "so vain."

What gives me joy? Driving in strange cities and getting lost. Eating turkey sandwiches for dinner and not some four-course chi-chi thing I can't even pronounce. Exercise brings joy—especially when it's over and I'm in the shower thinking, *I can't believe I hauled myself out there today.* I do like to water ski—to me it's really invigorating. It's about control. Power. Strength. Yet I have this fantasy that I'm actually flying over water, which is a brief moment of completely letting go.

And that's the point of your favorite things: They transport you to a giddy place inside that most of us card-carrying adults avoid, because we feel guilty in indulging in whims. Kids are supposed to have whims, and grown-ups are supposed to "get the job done." Kids can tinker, but we have to "toe the line," "keep it on course" . . . and other mundane, trite slogans that sound like drudgery. Whims seem too frivolous.

Yes, you think, someday you'll get back to those joyful things, but only after you get done with work things, home things, kid things—but as we all know, there's never enough time for everything. So the joyful parts of life get placed on some sort of permanent hold. Maybe forever.

I'm not waiting until I'm 80 and retired to water ski. I need an infusion of joy *right now*. Likewise, what prize is there in denying yourself the things that make you feel like life is an awesome adventure?

Indulge—but save the last brownie for me.

SIMPLE THOUGHT:

"The other day a really great song came on the radio, so I pulled the car over, got out, and started dancing. Why not just live in the moment, especially if it has a good beat?"

— Goldie Hawn

helpful things

I read that Denzel Washington has a Christmas ritual: Each year, he takes his wife and children to a soup kitchen in New York City and spends the day helping others.

He doesn't do this so the press can take photos of him dishing out mashed potatoes, or to promote his latest movie. Denzel does it because, as he says, "My kids have so much, and it's the only way I can teach them that there is a responsibility in this life that comes with being lucky. You give some of yourself to others."

He's right. Every year I go to a children's hospital in Knoxville, Tennessee, for a special breakfast with the kids. To tell you the truth, before I met these kids, I always felt really bad that I wasn't doing anything charitable. All my friends do great things. I'd hear, "I deliver food on Thanksgiving," or "I work in an animal shelter," and I always felt like such a bum because I didn't know where to start. Then I realized that the best way to give back is to do what you do best—but do it for others. For instance, I always play piano on the Children's Miracle Network telethon, and I play a concert for these kids in the hospital. It makes them feel special, which is the point.

It's also amazing that something so simple to me could be so helpful to others; by the same token, maybe you have a skill or hobby that could fit the same slot. It's funny how easy it actually is to give yourself to other people. The kids in Knoxville come to breakfast and I play. It's simple. Uncomplicated.

And I know that one morning with those children gives me much more than it gives them.

SIMPLE THOUGHT:

"I've learned to appreciate what my grandmother told me when I was younger, which was simple. When you were born, your life is like an empty vase. All your life people put flowers in your vase. You should give the flowers back because you don't want to leave this earth with your vase full."

— Irma P. Hall

learning things

You read these stories about 90-year-old women who go back to college. Obviously, they're not dreaming of getting ahead in the workplace. They are—gasp!—there to learn. Remember as a kid how you couldn't wait to get out of school and stop learning? It all seemed so boring and stupid. And did we ever really use algebra in our everyday lives? Well, not in my life. If I ever got a piece of paper that said "x" is to "y" over "z," I'd probably faint. Or call my accountant to figure it out.

But there's a funny thing about learning. As an adult, you long for a whole different type of education. And it's not in the hallowed walls of some lecture hall (although I have a few friends who have gone back to school and love it).

Dyan Cannon says that her best teacher is a 90-year-old woman named Rosie who goes with her to the Los Angeles Lakers games. Suddenly this senior citizen wanted to learn more about basketball. "She gets all dressed up really cute and comes to every game, no matter if she has aches or pains that day," says Dyan. "She knows the rules. She knows the players. She's thrilled by sports at this age." Yes, Rosie knows what few of us can figure out: It's very simple and thrilling to expand your mind.

A friend of mine is a writer. Each week he goes to a class of six people who get together to read each other their stories. They also assign a book to mull over each month. He loves it. He can't get enough of it. He's 36 years old and basically . . . back in English class.

I miss learning. Why is it that we get to age 22, receive a college diploma, and then shut the book on knowledge? Why don't we cultivate new interests and take them seriously? It's so very simple.

My mom might kill me, but I'm going on the record to say that she's a fantastic storyteller and writer. She actually sends in stories for my Website. I'm like, "Mom, this is really great." But she just pooh-poohs the whole thing and says, "Oh, it's just this little idea, James. This sort of stuff just flows out of me." She should have become a famous writer, but it wasn't easy for a single mother taking care of two kids. Writing was her hobby—it came after cooking dinner, doing the wash, and hounding us about our homework. Taking a writing class would have been considered a foolish waste of time, but she would have loved it.

But now she works at a library, and she's surrounded by what she loves. She keeps learning about the written word, and she continues to write in her spare time. It's inspiring.

Yet most of us don't allow ourselves enough time to keep learning. It just doesn't seem practical. We live in a time where everything has to produce tangible results. What if I learned about ancient Egypt? What would I do with that information? What if I took a poetry class? It's not like I'm going to become a famous poet. But that's just it—most people feel they can only do something if there's a larger result. For them, doing something in life is all about two things: If someone else notices and if they can use it to make a buck.

Knowledge doesn't work that way. Isn't your own motivation to learn enough?

Jodie Foster has repeatedly said that she doesn't regret having left Hollywood for four years to attend Yale. "That knowledge is with me for the rest of my life," she says.

So take a class that might inspire you. Learn something that might make you better than you thought you could be.

SIMPLE THOUGHT:

"I never let schooling interfere with my education."

— Mark Twain

the fear thing

I'm a very shy person. And people just don't get it. They'll say, "Yeah right, Jim, you're shy—and you're on a stage in front of 4,000 people. Tell us another good one."

Honestly, it's so strange. I feel very comfortable on that stage. My brain can somehow deal with looking out into a sea of faces. I'm not afraid. But get me on a date with just one person and I'm terrified. I'm like Linus without a security blanket—which is a 1,000-pound wooden musical instrument that doesn't easily fit into a car. Meeting new people, even at my age, sends me off into this fearful place, which seems ridiculous. But it's true. I feel like the new kid in school.

Let's face it. We're all a little scared these days. Fear is a simple emotion, but it's also a useful one.

Starr Jones, one of the self-assured hosts of the morning TV show *The View,* says that one of her biggest fears was buying her first home. "It was so tough and so expensive that one day I found myself sitting in the middle of my bed crying from the stress. I just felt so overwhelmed and afraid," she recalls.

So Starr really examined the root of her fears. "Finally, I realized that I didn't have to do everything at once." By discovering the core of her anxiety, she says, "I could finally relax and let it go."

She wasn't afraid anymore.

I admire the fact that my good friend Donny Osmond has been so forthcoming in talking about his stage fright. I know it sounds odd, because he's been performing since he was a child, but Donny remembers that he was actually paralyzed with fear one night. He was starring in the critically acclaimed musical *Joseph and the Amazing Technicolor Dreamcoat* in Chicago, and he almost couldn't go on stage. His wife, Debbie, helped him pinpoint the core of his panic. "I felt like I had to be perfect every moment of my life," says Donny. "Debbie made me realize that my 'pretty good' was better than good enough. Just that realization helped me not only go on stage, but enjoy it without any fears."

Olivia Newton-John noticed a lump in her breast a few years ago—it turned out to be cancer. She was afraid that she would die. But since recovering—and thank God she's been cancer free for many years—she's turned her fear into a weapon. "Nothing will ever be as bad as hearing the news that you have cancer," Olivia says. "How could I possibly be afraid, then, when I sit down to write a song? How does it even compare? It's almost like facing my worst fear gave me a steely sort of determination to bulldoze my way through more mundane worries."

A final word on being afraid. At one time or another, everyone visits that scary place. You're convinced at two in the morning that someone is in the house—it's really your cat. You think that your boss is going to fire you—you end up getting a raise. You go to the doctor believing you have six months to live—you just need to have a benign mole removed. You get the idea. I personally believe that fear is a great motivator. Being afraid can even be healthy, as you really achieve something

grand when you get to the other side of
your worst nightmares.

**SIMPLE
THOUGHT:**

"Inspiration has no deadline."

— Alan Safier

instinctual things

If I'm in a good situation, with interesting people and ideas flowing, I have this sense of euphoria that quakes through my entire body—like when you were a child, and something thrilled you to the point that your blood actually tingled. Something clicks within me, and that little inner voice that I usually put on mute says, "Jim, this is totally right. These people belong in your life, and you belong in this moment with them."

Frankly, no one listens enough to their instincts. I call it "gut sense." And we should all give it more credit.

I'll tell you a goofy little story. On our

Christmas tour in 2000, Anne Cochran, Wendy Leonard (who is now my tour manager), Donny Osmond, and I were driving from a gig in Boston to New Hampshire. We were all in this little rental car on one of those gray, depressing, freezing December days. The deal was that we were all supposed to go on a flight. But backstage after the show, the four of us looked at each other and said, "Let's rent a car. It will be so much more fun."

It was a road trip for grown-ups. We're talking loud music. Laughter. Potato chips spilled between the rental seats. The only thing that separated us from teenagers on the same trip was that we paid for our gas with credit cards, and the kid behind the counter at the Amoco called me "sir." Ouch.

But back to the open road. At a certain point, it got a bit endless, so we stopped to eat. We're hunkered down in this cozy booth, in a Chili's, in the middle of freaking nowhere. I mean, it was some strip mall buried in the murkiness of Sticksville, USA.

Suddenly, you could hear a buzz building. Several people started whispering, "That's Donny Osmond! What is *he* doing here? At Chili's, in the boonies. And isn't that Jim Brickman with him?" I started to laugh. Anne and Wendy giggled. Donny roared. We were like high school kids about to be sent to detention, because we just couldn't stop cracking up for no reason. And it must certainly state *somewhere* in the grown-up handbook that that's a no-no.

Of all the places we went on that tour, that afternoon was the most fun we had. We could not stop acting like idiots. It was just one of those moments where our managers, spouses, and significant others didn't know where we were in the world. Our cell phones were left in the car. We didn't have a big master plan. Our gut sense told us to get in that car and drive. And the real thrill of it was asking this question: When is the last time you escaped your life?

Instinctually, it felt like the most right thing I'd done in a year. It wasn't about someone taking care of us, or about the way we were supposed to be treated. And because it was Chili's in suburbia, there was no reason why I would be there or why Donny would be there.

Finally, the waitress comes over and says, "Excuse me, hon. I have a bet with my manager. Are you . . ."

I said, "Nah."

Donny said, "I'm not either. But we get that all the time."

The waitress just scrunched up her nose and said, "Hon, I didn't think so. I couldn't imagine why those two guys would be at my station!"

This sent Wendy and Anne into more laughter spasms. And deep inside, it all felt right. We weren't playing at being adults. We were just being ourselves, which felt perfect. And perfection is a simple feeling, but not a common one these days.

That afternoon, it was about the love and laughter of friends . . . and those ribs, which were actually pretty perfect, too. My gut was telling me a few things as well— such as, enough with the hot sauce. Quite simply, I was happy.

The point is that you should listen to your instincts. They don't charge $200 an hour like a therapist, and you don't need a ten-cents-a-minute calling plan to afford them. Your instincts can tell you the big stuff, such as whom you should marry, what to do in a crisis, or whom you should trust. But they can also help you with the little things, such as, yes, you should put cheese on that burger, and, absolutely, you should allow your friends to steal you away on a cold winter afternoon.

SIMPLE THOUGHT:

"Don't wait for your ship to come in. Swim out to it."

— Unknown

the escape thing

I love to swim. I don't necessarily like the beach, because I can't just lie there—I'll turn into a human tomato. I don't even really like hot weather. It's all about the water for me.

So go jump in a lake—which I only say in the most polite way—for the best part will be losing yourself in a watery world that literally mutes the rest of your existence.

Water has always been a special part of my life. For me, it's about escape: I love big waves that capture my body and catapult me recklessly into their own foamy, swirling wake.

First, a little history lesson. My love

affair with water began while I was growing up, for my entire extended family lived in Virginia Beach, with my grandmother living right by the shore. We would spend summers there—which sounds great, but there was a price. You see, Granny was a bit of a tyrant. Once I got finished doing all my calisthenics (remember when we called it that?), building her a patio, and sweeping the garage, I'd be allowed to go AWOL, so I'd sneak away to the beach.

If you really think about it, swimming is all about freedom and escape. When you're in the water, there isn't a road map. There isn't a path. I can go in one direction—or another. I can allow myself to feel very heavy and sink to the bottom. It's like a blank slate—the possibilities are endless.

In fact, swimming is like the piano keyboard to me. When I sit down on that piano bench, I have no idea where I'm going to go, or where my hands will take me. It's very much the same in the water. There are no rules. And we live in a world that tells us how to get from point A to point B in exacting detail. It's a very complicated way to live. But in the ocean, no one is saying, "Hey, pal, here's what you have to do to pass go and collect your 200 bucks."

And how often in this life do we get to do anything devoid of orders? For instance, when I'm on tour, I get very precise schedules. I'm told, "Jim, be at this radio station at 11 A.M. And then be at this interview by noon. And we have a lunch meeting at one and a photo shoot at two. . . ." It's at this point that my brain longs to go into escape mode.

Every once in a while, I indulge myself. I remember one especially nippy winter day when I found myself at a concert in Oregon. The guy in the wetsuit on the beach that day—the one who looked like a cross between Jacques Cousteau and a human seal—was me.

My body submerged in the icy waters, and as I sank down, I could feel my daily pressures leaving my body. They started seeping out of my pores, and I felt free. And sometimes it just takes a simple act to let your own version of freedom ring.

SIMPLE THOUGHT:

"Think of what a better world it would be if we had cookies and milk about three o'clock every afternoon, and then lay down on our blankets for a nap."

— Barbara Jordan,
United States Congresswoman

creative things

In high school, my teachers would say, "Class, write a paper on history." I would write something weird like "The Music of the Civil War" and always get *D*'s. I'd say, "But Miss-Impossible-to-Please, you told me to write something about history." And the teacher would say, "Well, you should have written about what everybody else wrote about, Jim. Some boring battle would have been fine."

Isn't it supposed to be *my* viewpoint? I guess I've always been fighting to keep some sort of independent nature in a world of conformity, borders, and parameters. In my world, the more they try to box me in, the more I fight. I'm just not good at following along, which is why I play the piano and write music. I have the gift of being able to say what I want without being told how to do it. I can finally be creative.

Everybody has that creative side, whether you're building a sandcastle, writing a symphony, or cooking your world-famous spaghetti dish that no one else can quite figure out how to make. Please stop saying you're not talented. Mrs. Fields baked those same cookies when she was a housewife. Everybody said, "Man, these are really great cookies, Mrs. F. But I might need to try 20 or 30 more just to be sure." That's how she got started.

Everyone has a talent for doing something special. Many of us dismiss those talents as nothing special and think that's the end of it . . . maybe it's just the beginning.

Quite often, someone will attend one of my concerts and say, "Oh, man, I wish I could do what you do." And I always laugh and say, "Hey, what *do* you do? What's inside of *you* that's equally creative?"

I joke about not being from a creative or musical family, but remember that I told you that my mom is a great writer. She was always into writing letters, and still sends me formal notes in the mail. To her, it might seem silly; but to me, they're beautiful and special, and simply some of the most creative things I've ever read in my life. Of course, along with these great letters, my mom will also clip things out of the paper and write, "Hey, Jim, I saw this interview with Barbara Streisand. Do you know her?" Where she gets this stuff, I don't know.

My father is also very creative, and his imagination is endless. The man reads two books a day. It's because for the past 20 years, Dad has worked for the Ford Motor Company at their factory. When he has downtime, he likes to read. He knows everything about history and war and beautiful literature. He loves to read about art and music, and he can have the most creative conversations about any topic under the sun. It's his talent. And face it, anyone who lives by a good library can simply enroll themselves in my father's university of the mind.

Now might be a good time to mention that when I was growing up, Dad was a stockbroker. Speaking of simple things, he decided that the competitive rat race of making money and living by the final bell of the day wasn't for him. He wanted to have a real life, one where his hours at home weren't consumed with thoughts such as, "Where is my next client? How do I make more money? Will I be fired tomorrow?" So he quit, and he took the job at Ford where he can punch a time clock. But when he gets home, it's done.

He's also a very creative cook. Believe me, you never go hungry at my father's house. He likes to create meals that are works of art. I used to always say, "Dad, why don't you just become a chef? And open a restaurant, or write a cookbook? And go on *Oprah* and get your own cable show?"

But my father knows that you can be creative for yourself. He knows it's not about public acclaim, but private victories. He'll say, "Jim, if I become a chef, then my hobby, which I love, will turn into work, and I won't be as creative about it."

SIMPLE THOUGHT:

"I don't know anything about music. In my line, you don't have to know too much. You just play from your heart."

— Elvis Presley

quiet things

I really love to be in airplanes—to me, 30,000 feet in the air means no phones ringing, no beepers going off. I'm forced to be still. And because I'm around people all of the time, I really prize my quiet times. If I'm at home and there's no noise, it's heaven. I'm talking about the peaceful sound of no cars driving down the street, no massive construction projects, no one ringing the doorbell, asking, "Mr. Brickman, wouldn't you like to buy 200 boxes of Girl Scout cookies?"

I long for those tranquil moments of absolute nothing. And I think the reason I really like them is because the moment the world goes mute, my brain seems to open like a flower in the spring. I actually can feel little inner doors unlocking.

Look for the quiet moments. Whoever said it's pretty cool to go grocery shopping at midnight at a 24-hour market has the right idea. It's the same thing with movies. Give me a dark movie theater on a Tuesday afternoon at four o'clock when nobody else is there. I'd never go to a movie on a Friday night. If you see some guy who looks like me, it's the twin brother my mother conveniently never told me existed.

I hate the fact that there are no quiet spaces. I get dragged to the gym, and all I hear is the "thump, thump, thump" of loud music. The other day I went to this beautiful little café to have a nice cup of tea. And the most awful rap song was on in the background. I don't understand it.

Isn't there any peace? There's this juice place in L.A. that shall go nameless (but you know who you are). It's a health-conscious place where they push ginseng and extracts that do God knows what to your body. All I know is that the chocolate-banana shake tastes really good.

But here's the problem: I walk in, and there's this cement floor, really uncomfortable chairs, and the counter kids are screaming out the orders to each other. How is that helping my health or well-being? Yes, I'm drinking carrot juice, but my nerves are totally frayed—I'd rather commune with carrots in the peace and quiet of my kitchen.

SIMPLE THOUGHT:

*"Knowledge speaks,
but wisdom listens."*

— Jimi Hendrix

spiritual things

I like the word *faith:* faith in God, in yourself, in your family. It's such an important thing to believe in something these days.

First, let me give you a disclaimer. At this point in the book, I should be telling you about a terrible car accident where I escaped completely unharmed. Or the time when I was in a hospital room with a friend or loved one and I observed them taking their final breath. But I've actually been one of the lucky ones. Nobody's ever been sick around me. I mean, we're not even talking chicken pox, let alone far worse things. And I hate to bring attention to it because tomorrow . . . who knows? It's almost as if I'm waving a flag at fate and saying, "Whoops, you missed me."

And that's where faith comes in—my faith in a higher power. I credit my faith with why I've been so blessed with such a trouble-free life. And my faith tells me that eventually when times do get rough, I'll be guided through it if I continue to believe.

I'm at an age where friends' parents have died. My good friend Wendy has had such a rough time of it lately. It's been one thing after another—cancer, sickness, death. And since we're friends, we've talked all about how your faith is sometimes the only tool you have when the world makes no sense at all, and it just doesn't seem fair.

But all of us have or will have something difficult happen in our lives. And sometimes you need to just believe. Believe in something bigger than yourself. Believe in something good lurking just around the corner. Believe that after you close your eyes and wake up in the morning, it just might be all right.

Actor Kelsey Grammer is someone who knows these things to be true. His beloved sister was murdered, and his brother was killed in a shark attack. One wonders how anyone can cope with such tragedy in their life. "There's a song I love from Michael McDonald," Kelsey explains, actually singing a few lines of the tune.

The song's message is that people can *always* give up, so McDonald suggests that you make that your last option. It should be the 31st of your 31 flavors—your bargain-basement choice. Why not move on up with a little hope and a lot of belief? And if that seems impossible, a deep breath and a leap of faith can also do.

Kelsey goes on to say, "I guess I just

have a great sense of joy in life. Even in the darkest days, there was always something to look forward to tomorrow. And it's true that in our greatest adversity, we can sometimes find our greatest joy. But you can't find that joy alone. I think my faith in God has gotten me through the tough times. That faith tells me that the next day will come and there will be a reason to go on living."

An old friend of mine, Molly Shannon, found this to be true. When she was four years old, her family was coming home from a picnic when they were cut off by another driver. Her mother was killed before her eyes in a tragic accident that also injured her father and sister. A very young Molly was sent to wait for the news in the hospital waiting room. That's where she told her first joke. "I looked around that emergency room and saw people who might have it even worse than me," she says. "I knew it was my job to make them laugh. I don't know why I thought this, or where it came from inside of me. I felt like something was telling me what to do."

People talk to me about how music hovers on the fringes of faith. And this is as ethereal as I get, but sometimes I'll play something, and I truly wonder how this music came out of me. I really do sit there with my hands on the keys, and I feel like something or someone else is guiding them.

It comes so naturally. And people will say, "Oh, you must have practiced so hard." I'm almost embarrassed. I mean, obviously, I've practiced, but I don't feel like it's been a struggle. I'll just close my eyes in concert and the music simply flows. And I have to believe that there might be a higher reason why I'm supposed to share this thing with other people.

Fans will say, "Jim, your music helped

me through a really tough time. When my heart was really heavy, a certain piece made me feel lighter." I'm not that mystical, and it's hard to put it into words. But in those moments, I feel like the faith inside of me is being put to good use. I feel blessed.

SIMPLE THOUGHT:

"Unless you believe,
you shall not understand."

— The Bible

the me, me, me thing

Face it—the one person you never spend time with is yourself. It's almost too mind-boggling when you think of the questions that would immediately come up if you did: What would I mull over with myself? Would I find myself amusing? Would I have anything to talk about with me? Oh, no, I'm not making myself laugh. Am I a bore? And here's the big one: Would I even like myself? Or would I think, *Gosh, I wish I could dump this guy and find someone else's self who's a lot more fun.*

Okay, I'll stop. But you get the idea.

It's easy to ignore yourself. It's especially

easy when we're always racing, talking, doing, and going, which leaves little time for just *being*. But often people say to me, "I get lost in my head listening to your music." What I take that to mean is: (1) Hey, they like the music; and (2) I'm reconnecting people to themselves in a weird way.

Let me explain. I find it really hard to sit in a room by myself. I'd go crazy—certifiably nuts. I mean, have you ever tried to just sit in a chair and . . . drum roll, please . . . think? But the simple act of thinking is so helpful, because you might actually find yourself in those thoughts. And we're so busy doing a million things that we don't really have time to find ourselves.

Think about this: What do you really want from this life? Do you ever have a moment to just sit down and really focus on what you want to achieve during your time on the planet? Forcing yourself to answer such questions is rough, but necessary. For me, of course, it has to do with music. And now back to that very thing.

When people say, "Your music gets me through the day," I feel like I've been their invisible companion. Many people put on the music and it feels like somebody is there with them. And with that "invisible support system," they can let their mind go free and wander to otherwise unexplored places. Call it a mental Club Med vacation. You're the tour guide. Airfare doesn't even have to be included, because you can just close your eyes and go anyplace in your head.

It's not a bad thing to do some really deep meditation. It doesn't have to be as formal as sitting on your brown La-Z-Boy on the third recline notch and staring at the paint-chipped ceiling. Maybe, for instance, you're driving in your car, and the music playing starts to make you daydream—but not to the point where you don't notice that Mack truck in the distance. *Please be careful.* Anyway, let's say you're obeying the rules of the road, but "drifting" just a little bit, when suddenly you're sent to a place deep inside where you're thinking, *Huh, I never thought about that stuff.* The music isn't dredging up these feelings. It's more like a catalyst that takes you on a mental voyage.

I like to walk around my neighborhood in the canyons of Los Angeles, and I wish I could tell you that it's because I'm a nature freak. Nah, I go on these walks because the gym in Hollywood drives me crazy, and I live in a hilly neighborhood, so it's good "interval training," which is basically a fancy way of saying that you sweat a ton by running up the hill. It's really good for your heart, not to mention helpful for the hips.

I could never walk outside without

headphones and two or three CDs. Honestly, I'm afraid of what I would think. I'm almost afraid to have that time with myself because: (1) What would I really think about; and (2) Do I really want to think those things?

No, no, no! Let me repeat: *No!* Keep me away from myself.

You know what it's like when your brain gets a little bit too pushy. You start thinking, *Why am I with this person and not this other person? Why am I doing this with my work? When I'm 90, will I have all my hair and teeth?* (Insert a loud scream here.)

We live in a time of overstimulation.

There's not a moment when we're not "on something"—such as the TV, radio, CD player, or cordless whatever. I've gotten to the point where I can't take a bath for more than ten minutes—just me and some bub-bles—I also have to be on the phone, watching TV, or flipping through the pages of *Newsweek*. Suddenly, I'm not thinking about myself.

Maybe we're all a little afraid of our own thoughts. Maybe *afraid* is too big a word— we're just leery of them. So now I force myself to be alone with the one person I should know better than anyone—me. Try forcing yourself: Get on a stationary bike, or take a walk, *without any other stimulation than your own thoughts.* You'll be surprised at what comes to mind—and usually those are the important things.

I'll confess that I figured out this trick one day while I was way, way up in the canyons walking, and the most horrible thing on earth happened to me—the batteries in my Walkman died. And even a little battery prayer—"Please, spirit of Duracell, let them work"—didn't help. I was in a panic, wondering, *Oh my God,*

what am I going to think about for the next
20 minutes?

It was the beginning of self-discovery.

SIMPLE
THOUGHT:

"My greatest strength is common
sense. I'm a standard brand, like
Campbell's soup or Baker's chocolate."

— Katharine Hepburn

little things

I'm an uncle. It's a scientific, medically proven, statistically agreed upon fact that I have the most beautiful nephew in the world. Okay, well, maybe *all* the data isn't in. Sue me for being prejudiced.

Let me describe baby Thomas Brickman for a minute. First of all, my nephew looks so much like my brother and me that it's as if he's the mini-version of us, without all of our worries, responsibilities, and pressures. In his clear green eyes, all you see is hope, clarity, and wonder—although sometimes I know he's wondering if Uncle Jim can really handle the dirty diapers, and maybe it would be best to get Mommy in on the deal.

As for burping, I defer when it comes to anything involving projectile mucus.

I take whatever time I have and go see Thomas, who happens to live in New Jersey. It isn't easy, but I don't want to miss anything. Each time I see him as it is, it's like he's been in a time machine. Babies change so rapidly that you just have to say, "I'm not going on vacation. I'm not going to spend two days chilling out in a hotel room after a concert. I'm going to be an uncle."

I marvel at parents who have to make decisions on a daily basis about how much time to spend with their kids, versus work or relationships. It's gut-wrenching. The best parenthood advice I can give comes from a friend of mine, who insists that no matter who's on the phone, or what deal is going down, it doesn't matter—he absolutely stops *everything* when his daughter walks in the door from school. For the next 15 minutes, the Pope or the President could be on hold; the FBI could be knocking on the door needing my friend's help with matters of national security—they can wait. Instead, he's asking, "How did you do on your math test? Was that rotten Billy mean to you today?"

It's precious, necessary time. And 20 years from now, when his daughter is grown, I know my friend won't be saying, "Gee, I wish I could have been on the phone with that client from Tulsa for 15 more minutes."

Me? I'm new to this kid stuff. So it's not simple to me at all. I'm even a little nuts about it. The responsibility hits me like a slab of concrete. In fact, I remember meeting my nephew the week he was born— paralysis almost set in. First, I'd never really held a baby, which I guess is a typical guy thing. I really didn't know what to do.

My first thoughts were about this fragile being. Questions weighed heavily on me, such as: *What happens if Uncle Jim drops the baby? Do I jump off a building? Does my mother ever speak to me again? Do I change last names?* Weird things go through your mind at moments like these.

So I remember looking at my baby nephew and then making a big confession to my brother and his wife. I told them about the last time I dropped a baby. You see, as a teenager, I needed some cash, so I got talked into baby-sitting. And the victims of my ineptitude were a little baby, and a three-year-old who was more interested in eating lint than bothering me. I sat the little baby on the couch and gave him a command as if he were a puppy: "Okay, stay! I'm just going to go in the kitchen for a minute."

Thump! That's what I heard while I was making myself a sandwich. My first thought was, *Wait just a minute. I told him to stay.*

Thank God, nothing happened. But as I told my sister-in-law the story, you could see her eyes open wide. Her thoughts seemed to say, *Let's keep the kid away from Jim. Until he's 18.*

I've since proven myself with Thomas. If he's on the couch, I'm like a human fence around him. In my less paranoid moments, I can't help but stare at my nephew and think, *That's what my child would look like if I had one.* My kid would also have that little lip thing going—it's not an overbite, but a little Brickman lip curl. And then I realize: Thomas is the next generation. It's us for a new millennium.

I envy my brother and his wife, Connie. Their commitment to Thomas is inspiring. The way they take care of him is so unselfish.

I'm not in the mode right now to think about my own carbon copy. At least not yet. But Thomas gets me thinking about it.

Because he's the future.

Because he's beautiful.

Because last December, he sat silently during my two-hour concert and didn't cry once. I prefer to think that the music was peaceful to him—my brother says he just had a huge meal. Still, in order to encourage a future musical genius, I just bought him a cool mobile that makes all sorts of music. I also got him a tape recorder. And I can't wait to teach him how to play the piano.

SIMPLE
THOUGHT:

*"At the end of your life,
you will never regret not having
passed one more test,
not winning one more verdict,
or not closing one more deal.
You will regret time not spent
with a husband, a child,
a friend, or a parent."*

— Barbara Bush

resourceful things

Your home is a wondrous place. You just don't realize it.

I hear from people, "I love to play music, but I can't be serious about it. I don't have access to a recording studio. I couldn't write a song. I don't have the money for fancy equipment."

I'll bet you can do it. I record my music at home. It's very simple: I walk in the living room, turn on a tape recorder, and play. It's like a studio environment, but it's also like a million other homes out there because there are wood floors. My other recording tools? I have a blanket and a pillow inside the piano to buffer some of the sound that bounces back from the ceiling.

Do you want high-tech equipment or bottom-line basics? In my case, it's the latter. My recording engineer comes over and says, "Hey, Jim, do you need that pillow on the couch?" I'll say no, so he takes the thing and puts it in my piano. Then he takes the cushion part of my lounge chair and puts it on the floor to get rid of echoes. I have a digital audio deck and two great mikes. You'll never know from listening to my new CD that I could have been doing laundry at the same time I was recording it. Or lasagna could have been bubbling in the oven.

The point is that we make so many complicated excuses for not doing things. Whatever happened to a little simple ingenuity? For instance, you don't need an artist's studio to paint if you have a kitchen table, a sink, and a few bowls to mix colors.

You don't need to recreate the love scene in *Ghost* to dabble in pottery—get a hunk of clay and start molding. You don't need to take expensive writing courses to start a book—grab a piece of paper and a pen.

Of course, it comes down to a little creativity and a lot of motivation. The creativity is inside all of us. The motivation is rougher. Face it—it's hard to rev yourself up to do anything these days beyond the typical daily grind of eat-work-sleep. It's even harder to psyche yourself up at home when you could be spending your days in pursuit of loftier endeavors . . . such as all of those reruns on Nick at Night.

How do I write a song? I don't get up in the morning and give myself a pep talk. I'm not like a high school kid who has a term paper due today and starts to mutter, "Okay, Jim, you've gotta do this. You have no choice."

In fact, for the past couple days, I haven't played at all. Then it hit me: I need to play. I want to play. Last year on Easter, I got a few nice invitations for dinner. But I knew it was the perfect day to record: It was quiet and peaceful—no cars were racing down the street, no construction workers were barking orders. So I just put my pillow in the piano and allowed my energy to flow. It was that easy.

SIMPLE THOUGHT:

"Some people look at the world and say why. Some people look at the world and say why not."

— George Bernard Shaw

joyful things

My father is a very charming man. He's the type of guy who will say, "I'm going to the grocery store for some milk," and then an hour and a half later, we'll start to wonder, "Did Dad get kidnapped by terrorists? Maybe we should call the FBI. Where the hell is he?" After what seems like a decade, he'll finally walk in the door with a big smile and say, "Oh, James, I got into this conversation with the girl at the checkout counter at the grocery store. She was asking me about my travels and my linguini choices. We had such a fun chat." I'm like, "What! We thought you were in a ditch. Can't you call?"

I sound like the parent.

I've recently been thinking about why these little scenes with my father bother me so much. In a nutshell, he's able to do things on a whim. And I'm not.

Normally, I wouldn't even notice the checkout girl. I'd walk in, plop down some money, lose my sunglasses or keys, and haul my purchases out to my car—pausing only to pick up my canned corn after the flimsy paper bag bursts in the parking lot. (Insert a few swear words here.)

When I was a child, my father always told me, "James, you're way too serious. Have some fun. Experience life's joys."

And I'd think, *Thanks, Dr. Joyce Brothers—I mean, Dad—for that great nugget of advice. But I have to work. I don't have time for fun, so get off my back. Oh, and have a nice day.*

So a little while ago, I'm on the phone

with my father—who had just returned from a cruise—and he starts in on me again. "James, you're going to take some time off, aren't you? You *are* making time for fun, right? Why don't you ever fit in some time to just have *fun,* son?"

Fun, fun, fun. To me, it was the new "f" word, and I used to bristle each time he used it. But then it dawned on me: My father is right.

Here's the problem, however: As adults, we're not very good at having fun anymore. We don't even know how to begin. Whims? When's the last time one of *those* was part of your day? I even did a little research on it. Nothing scientific—I called up a few of my friends and nonchalantly asked, "What's the last thing you did for the sheer fun of it?" And I got answers such as, "Well, I rested for ten minutes on Sunday after cleaning the gutters all day. Does that count?"

No, it doesn't. Maybe we're afraid to have fun. Joy? *Oy.* And we ruin the very concept by treating our fun like a job. You plan your vacation with military-type precision. You map out each moment—God forbid there's any spontaneity, because that won't do. But then, you go to check in to your swanky hotel, and that family of 12 thinks it's adorable that their kids are running around and screaming at the top of their lungs. There's also an insurance convention going on, and it takes an hour to finally make it to your room. Your blood boils. The stress kicks in. Immediately, your adult brain gets into gear and thinks, *I'm paying big bucks and this is not fun! Little Suzy at the table next to me is having a hissy fit. This is all wrong. This isn't what I planned! This isn't* (insert Dad's "f" word)!

So I won't go on those planned vacations anymore. Sorry, Club Whatever. And before I get a call from my father about the lack of joy and frivolity in my life, let me at least give him this disclaimer: I've found fun in a different way. And no, this isn't the racy part of the book. But it does involve quickies.

On the spur of the moment, I'll get in my car and drive a few hours to the mountains for the weekend. Maybe I don't even have a reservation at Cabin Unwind and Eat Tree Bark. I certainly don't have a plan, but suddenly it's the "f" word, because it's an adventure. And as adults, how many times do we get to have an adventure?

When I was a kid, each day was an adventure. My trusty bike and some woods were better than going to Neverland any day. In my mind, there was danger, excitement, and the unknown—not to mention poison ivy around every bend.

I'm asking: Do you really need to fly 20 hours to Hawaii to sit in the sun? We've all come up with this concept that the more exotic it is, the more fun it must be, which just isn't true. I've found that my home is just as good a place to get a tan and relax. The lemonade tastes just as delicious from my own fridge as it does when it costs four dollars and comes with a flimsy paper umbrella. The "spa" is just a bathtub—but it's still relaxing.

Chez Jim doesn't get written up in *Travel and Leisure* magazine. But it really *is* a fine place to unwind. It's exactly a three-minute drive to the mountain conservatory by my home. The minute I walk out of my car, I'm in the woods. If I took a picture and said, "Where is this?" you might say, "Is it Oregon? Is it the rain forest? Do I see those *Survivor* contestants in the background?"

It's my own backyard.

SIMPLE THOUGHT:

"Everything has been figured out, except how to live."

— Jean-Paul Sartre

financial things

Jay Leno didn't have lunch the other day. Not because he's on a diet—he went to a McDonald's, but they weren't having any big-meal deals. Says Jay, "Maybe it's because my parents grew up in the Depression, but something inside of me clicked. I said, 'Well, I can wait until they're having 39-cent cheeseburgers, because that's a good deal.'"

This is a guy who makes really big bucks. But he says, "I've never spent a dime of my *Tonight Show* money. It's all in the bank or in investments. I live off my stand-up career, which means I don't live a show-biz lifestyle. I live a *real* lifestyle. And I'm happier for it."

I know what Jay means. So does Sally, my mom, who will pick it up right here:

"In Shaker Heights, Ohio, where James grew up, there were many wealthy people, and his friends were often given life's every extravagance. But coming from a divorced family, it was different for us. If my sons wanted spending money, they had to work for it. James delivered gifts for a delivery service. He swept floors at a recording studio. He learned the value of a dollar. Believe me, the boys were better for it. They became responsible for themselves. It was character building.

"But it wasn't always easy. I remember this very fancy lady ran the local dance school. We couldn't afford for James to keep taking lessons there, so she gave him a scholarship. But before the final dance, she called me and said, 'By the way, James can't bring a date because he's on financial aid. If you don't pay full fare, you don't get extra considerations.'"

It hurt at the time, but it taught us a nice lesson. (Hello, it's Jim again.) The moral is that if you're going to do something nice, don't put qualifications on it. It's like selling a car without the tires. And if you're doing something good that involves money, give the person with less funds some respect. Respect shouldn't come with a price tag— basic humanity isn't for sale.

Eventually, Mom taught us to excuse ourselves from people who seemed to only care about splitting people into two teams: the "haves" and "have nots." We knew something that their money couldn't buy: A wallet didn't mean compassion, and a lot of zeroes in your bank account doesn't mean much more than you're getting a free blender from the bank as a thanks. I learned that during the happiest moments of my life when I was a "have not."

When I was in college, I lived in this apartment with a roommate. It was a one-bedroom job with twin beds. We'd lived in the dorm together, and this wasn't much bigger. You could barely turn around in the bathroom. The kitchen—and I loosely use that term—wasn't much more than a hot plate and a $10 toaster that would nicely blacken your bagels.

But I can't stop remembering how happy I was back then—I was filled with hope and promise, and the world seemed to be a place with endless possibilities. My happiness had nothing to do with a bulging wallet, or where I lived, or if I had a decent car. I did, however, have a very nice Schwinn bike.

A lot of times people mix up the passion for making music with the dough. Yes, there are people who want to be stars and end up making millions of dollars. I'm sure that's a nice ambition, but it isn't mine. I've come to know that the good things never really start with dollar signs. The way to make money is to do what you love. Then if you're very lucky it might turn into something that rewards you in many ways—one of them being monetary.

I'd play piano for free. I know you don't believe it, but it's true. Music is who I am. Bill Gates loved tinkering on computers, and he did all right for himself. Time and time again, you hear stories like the one Jennifer Lopez tells—as a kid, she spent half her life in a darkened movie theater, wishing she was Maria from *West Side Story*. Regardless of her incredible stardom and success, acting and music are in her soul.

All of us have talents we can develop for the sheer love of it and not for the paycheck. If later you become a millionaire for your fudge recipe, then send me a thank-you note and a T-shirt. Oh, and something with lots of nuts, of course.

SIMPLE THOUGHT:

"Money doesn't talk, it swears."

— Bob Dylan

the rejection thing

When I was in advertising, I was working on a commercial for a top burger chain that I can't mention, because I don't need any calls from their lawyers.

Anyway, I walked in to this editing session, and all the ad people were having this huge yelling and screaming match, because for their commercial, the pickles weren't big enough, the burger looked a bit small in comparison to the tomato slices, and if some genius didn't fix it, then for God's sake, the onions would be really overwhelming. I bit my lip not to laugh. But my impulse to chuckle was short-lived, because I then heard a few words I'll never forget.

Some blowhard yelled, "And the music sounds like something Elmer Fudd wrote in his spare time."

Yes, it's okay to feel my pain. I can still remember that feeling. It's when your stomach drops a few hundred feet, your heart starts doing an internal mambo, and your head begins to ache, even though you're not the type to get migraines.

But the insults didn't stop there. The same putz went on to say, "The music is too cute. This isn't a cartoon!"

The ad people were ruthless. My theory is they're so "up front" because they would really rather be writing music or books, but their fancy offices and designer ties seem to give them a license to wield their frustration as a superpower. They're the kryptonite to your Superman. And if any ad execs are reading this book, I'm sorry. Of course, I don't mean *you*. Just your colleagues.

When I first started writing jingles, I often heard these words: "Jim, we really hate this!" Actually, in many ways, it helped me. Every bit of rejection added a sort of Teflon coating to me. It's true what they say about developing a thick skin. Now if I walk in to my record label, I'll look around the room at these music bigwigs and say, "Hi, you guys. When I say this, I'm actually serious—tell me what you think of this song."

There are a few bits of encouragement I can pass on here. And I say this from my heart.

First of all, if you're rejected, please don't give up your dream. I had a friend who was a photography student at a major university. She was a great photographer, but a certain "top" professor simply didn't like women. He gave her a tough time all semester, until she ultimately changed her major to business. She completely gave up and allowed one opinion to crush a lifelong dream.

If I would have given up every time someone told me I'd never make music professionally, I'd probably be sitting in some ad exec's office today hearing, "Your music makes the hot dog feel less significant than the mustard."

Singer Richard Marx was turned down by 12 record companies before he had an international hit record. Sylvester Stallone was told by most of the major studios that *Rocky* was a dumb idea for a movie and no one would ever go see it. It won an Oscar for the best picture of 1976.

The point is, there are no rights and wrongs—it's all up to interpretation. You may like licorice; I can't stand it. You may like Madonna; I'm not into it. I like sweet; you may like salty. Fruity, forget it—but I know there are people who savor those sour apple candies. Give me chocolate M&Ms.

But it's still cool that there's a variety of foods that will clog your arteries and ruin your teeth. Obviously, everyone has different tastes. And someone rejecting you on any level—professional, personal (and we'll get to that stuff in a minute), or snack food-wise—can be dealt with in a simple way. They don't share your same tastes. Period.

Some people at my record company are always on me. They'll say, "Jim, we think you need a hipper image. We don't really like hearing you tell the story on stage about how you learned to play piano on a piece of felt before your mother could afford to buy you a real instrument."

So I changed my act. I started skipping the felt story. Then after the shows, I'd be talking to fans backstage, and over and over again, I'd hear, "It was a great show, but how come you didn't tell the felt story? I told my husband, 'Wait till you hear this part about how he learned to play music.'"

In everyone's life, you'll hear, "Well, we just don't like such-and-such." I suggest you hit these cynics with a simple response. Just say, "Okay, what would you prefer?" I bet you'll hear these words, "Well, I dunno." And then say back to them, "Well, until you do know, I'll continue to do it my way."

You can be rejected for so many things: You're a bad cook, or a sloppy kisser. Which brings me to critics, which I've saved for the end of this chapter. Talk about rejection. I've read, "Jim's music is so syrupy." Or this is a good one: I recently got slammed by a journalist (of course, my mom cut the review out of the paper and sent it to me) who wrote, "Jim Brickman does the most vanilla music I've ever heard in my life."

I'm like, *I love vanilla*. I put vanilla in everything. I even put it in my protein shakes. I have vanilla candles. I know a lot of people who love vanilla, too. My take was that it wasn't a criticism of *me*—it was simply an endorsement for vanilla lovers everywhere.

SIMPLE THOUGHT:

"There is more stupidity than hydrogen in the universe, and it has a longer shelf life."

— Frank Zappa

comfortable things

I'll confess that my closet consists of two pairs of jeans. There's the pair I wear at home, which has a few rips in them, and the nicer pair (no rips) that I wear to radio stations and meetings.

Yes, I have a few versions of dress clothes that I wear onstage—but mostly, it comes down to one good black shirt and one blue one. If critics or fans are more interested in what I'm wearing than what I'm playing, I'm in big trouble.

I'm lucky that it starts with the music for most of my fans. It's not about my geeky shirt or whom I'm dating. Or if my name was in *The National Enquirer* last week because I was abducted by aliens. Oh, that never happened. Trust me.

And it doesn't matter to people who like my music that I wasn't at a premiere last week and photographed by *People* magazine, who would never want to take my picture because I'm dressed totally wrong. The "fashion police" might say, "Jim, wasn't that the same pair of jeans you wore six years ago at the only other premiere you've ever attended in your life?"

I should probably care more than I do about these things, but I don't. Wouldn't you rather be thought of as witty, clever, smart, or talented than best dressed? What does "best dressed" even say about you, other than that you're good at shopping?

Not that I want to be critical of those who love to shop—it's a hobby. It's just someone else's taste of how to spend an afternoon.

In fact, here's a funny story. My good friend Anne Cochran always looks so put together. Even if we're on a midnight red-eye flying to Hong Kong, she looks like she could do a fashion magazine layout. And then there's me: I'm the one in a T-shirt and jeans. Hey, it's not that bad, except for one time on a flight to Hawaii, I dared to wear the sweats. Of course, that's when the flight attendants swarmed me and wanted to take my picture.

Oh, well. To Anne, dressing up makes her happy and comfortable. As for me, give me my stretched-out Cleveland Indians sweat pants. I wrote a lot of songs on my new album, wearing them as inspiration. Why not put a maximum on comfort? Sorry, Armani—I'll take my radio station shirt from the Philippines any day. It's the one I've washed so many times that it's actually dissolving before my very eyes. When it even comes out of the washer at all, barely in one piece, I'm like, "Thank you, thank you, thank you."

It's really about what makes you feel comfortable and at ease in your world. If it's pearls and cashmere, fantastic. If it's faded blues and a baseball cap, I'm with you. Comfort comes in all forms. It might be eating meat loaf with a big squirt of ketchup. It might be Dairy Queen on a hot summer night, with that twisty cone that always melts all over your fingers before you make it to the car.

As for me, this dumb Philippines shirt has a connection to my world. It isn't just like, "Oh, I bought this plain green shirt at the discount store—who cares?" I went to this special place, and the shirt is a nice reminder of something that I've accomplished in my life. It reminds me that people zillions of miles away might not speak

English—but they listen to my music, and they invited me to their country. There's a comfort factor in knowing that I accomplished something big. Which is why I love that shirt.

Mr. Blackwell, leave me alone. Go pick on Pamela Anderson or something.

As for the rest of my house, I'll admit that it's pretty coordinated. But it's also very simple and comfortable. It's not even cluttered. My advice is to get rid of your junk. I've never felt more at ease in my life than when I finally allowed myself some room to breathe. I'll admit that I was as much of a pack rat as anyone else. But you get to this point where your life is just about chaos. You can't even relax in your own home because there's this constant pressure of thinking, *Okay, I gotta get rid of this stuff. I gotta give it the heave-ho. . . . But I like that cracked blue teapot that's probably covered*

*in lead-based paint. It's still functional, even
if it's poisoning my friends and me.*

I gave my life a whole new comfort level
by adopting a different way of living.
Basically, if a few months—not years, but
months—go by and I don't wear it, or if I
don't like it enough to buy it again, then I get
rid of it. I make two piles: There's an emotional pile and a useful pile. I kiss the emotional pile good-bye and send it off to the Jim
Brickman Memorial Stuff Museum in the sky.

Good-bye, good riddance.

Oh, maybe you're wondering what has
hit my emotional pile in the last few weeks.
I had this shirt from when I ran in a
Cleveland 10K marathon. This was from the
one week in my entire life when I was imag-
ining myself as the male Flo Jo. You could
literally see through the shirt, as I sometimes
wore it to bed. Occasionally, other people
exclaimed in horror, "You're wearing that

rag to bed?!" I always responded with a sincere gaze and these words: "I'm sorry, and I don't know why I must wear this to bed. But I must."

So you can see the emotional connection. And the comfort level. But I can proudly say that the other day I put the shirt out of its misery. I realized that I do have about 100 other ratty shirts . . . which was some small solace.

Next time you're in town, check it out—I'll be in my sweat pants when I answer the door.

SIMPLE THOUGHT:

"Fill what's empty, empty what's full, and scratch where it itches."

— The Duchess of Windsor, discussing the secrets of a happy life

emotional things

So, you want to break me down and make me cry. I have to confess that the last time my eyes welled up with tears was because . . . my sofa has this rough edge, and I caught my toe on it.

For more poignant tears that don't include any cuss words, just throw *Field of Dreams* on the VCR. I can't handle the moment at the end when Kevin Costner plays catch with his father, who's young again. Excuse me. Just thinking about them saying, "I love you, son," "I love you, Dad," makes me want to get a Kleenex. Sniff, sniff. I also love this movie because it deals with unresolved family issues and how you should deal with them. You really should tie up loose ends whenever you get the chance.

An Affair to Remember also gets me—at the end, when she's in the wheelchair. Much of it is the music. It touches a nerve with me.

I love the fact that movies can still make me cry. We live in a time when we don't allow ourselves to be emotional. When was the last time you broke down and wept? And did you feel guilty about it because now you're a grown-up? We're supposed to be strong, sure, and steadfast. And that sounds good . . . but a lot of times it's easier said than done.

It pains me to watch my friend Anne Cochran go through some very emotional issues with her kids. She has to leave them with her husband in Cleveland to go on the road with me, and it tears her apart. She wants to sing, but she also wants to be a mom. She wants to be with the audience *and* be in her kitchen. Consequently, if she's one place, she wants to be in the other. The bottom line is that there are no easy answers. There might not be an answer at all. And I've seen it reduce her to tears. "My children are my passion, but I also love music," says Anne. "And even if I'm gone for just one night, I know I'm missing the little things at home. Yes, the kids will still look the same 24 hours later. No one will go off to college, but maybe my nine-year-old son will hit a baseball, or play in the snow, or kick a soccer ball. And that makes me cry, because I don't want to miss even one moment of his childhood. It's so fleeting."

I can always tell when the conflict is bubbling up in Anne. I just know by the look on her face. Sometimes it's right before she goes on stage and her kids call her. I see her eyes well up with tears, but I tell her to use it in her performance. At that moment, 1,000 miles away from home, it's the only thing she can do. We have a song called "If I Could," which is about protecting your children and being there for them. Sometimes I'll be playing and I look over at Anne during the song, and she's crying. But it's almost therapeutic—the song is a way to remind her that her emotions aren't silly or frivolous. This stuff is important.

As a card-carrying baby boomer, how do you handle tough emotional moments? There's drinking and pills. We've seen how that didn't work for some of our friends.

I handle it with a piano. If I'm upset, I'll sit down and really take it out on those keys. Maybe you garden and can get through the tough moments by literally attacking the ground. And sometimes life is full of so many dirty tricks that you don't know what to do. It seems obvious, but sometimes the best thing to do in an emotional moment is to do the first thing that comes to mind—if it's legal and not self-destructive.

Once in a while, it's okay to eat the pan of brownies if it makes you feel better. It's okay to sit in the bathtub for two hours and cry, or listen to your favorite song and crank the volume up to ten. For me, I listen to Carly Simon. Her old records take me to a place of happiness, and it makes me think of the way I looked at my life way back when and how it's all turned out for me. It reminds me of choices I've made—good and bad. Likewise, I love The Carpenters and Fleetwood Mac—these are artists I listened to growing up, and they transport me to a different place.

Please, allow yourself some kind of release, even if it involves eating the whole tub of Cool Whip. A Snickers bar can be very therapeutic. Whatever works for you, whatever makes you feel as if a pin has been stuck inside the stress balloon you've been building up inside. Letting your emotions out is a simple notion. But the reason people our age have ulcers, stomach problems, and migraines is that we bottle it up inside until something just involuntarily bursts.

Let it out.

SIMPLE THOUGHT:

"If you are going through hell, keep going."

— Winston Churchill

romantic things

Yep, we just got to my real favorite thing—romance. Not that I'm Casanova by any means. Please. If you ever saw me fumble to ask someone out on a date, you might think, *Wait, this is the guy called America's Romantic Piano Sensation?* In my own defense, let me repeat what should be self-evident to all compact vehicle owners: I just can't bring the piano with me everywhere. It doesn't fit in the car. You can't roll it into the multiplex. So it's not so easy when I'm on my own without my good-luck charm, which happens to weigh more than 1,000 pounds.

But you learn—and you ask for tips. Romance is such a tricky thing these days, and there's no easy place to begin. Wait . . . there *is* an easy place. Let's start with Valentine's Day. I know I have a song called "Valentine," and I'm glad if you like it. But I need to make a little confession: I'm bad at Valentine's Day. The choices are so confusing—do you give candy or flowers? Should the card say "I love you" or "I like you"? And frankly, no one wants a Hallmark sentiment that reads, "You're one hell of a good person."

I think we put way too much pressure on ourselves for these forced romantic holidays. It's almost like you're being set up to fail. You know those little candy hearts that taste like chalk and contain a message like "Be Mine"? They should really say, "Loser, you should have bought jewelry." Or "Dinner at Arby's means divorce papers in the morning."

What else can I say about matters of the heart? Well, a friend of mine is very happily married—which is such a huge accomplishment in this day and age—and he says that each time he feels like he's taking his beloved wife for granted, he reminds himself to treat her like he did during the third month of their courtship.

It's such great and simple advice. You don't want to relive the first month of dating, where you're pretending to be a NASA astronaut and she claims to have been the second runner-up to Miss America. Sure, a few white lies rarely hurt, such as when you later confess that you teach science and she works at a makeup counter at Macy's. No real harm done there. And the second month of dating is still about not acting like your real self—because your normal self doesn't really have sex six times a day. But

SIMPLE THINGS

hey, when you're swept up in the thrill and
newness of it all, miracles do happen.

Month three of dating means that the
blinders are off, but the awe factor is still
there. You honestly feel lucky and blessed
to be with this person, and you're still
amazed that they like you back. And you
should still be hauling the flowers home.

Oh, since we're on the topic of foliage,
let's cut right to the chase. Everyone loves
flowers, but some people (men, especially)
just don't get it. I hear from my buddies this
familiar tale of woe: "Do I have to spend 50
bucks on expensive roses? And if I do, I'll
only do it on her birthday." But here's a tip
from the Secret Handbook of Womankind:
People with two X chromosomes (meaning
girl types) are thrilled to get even the $5
bouquet from the supermarket—which you
can purchase while buying hot dog buns
and windshield-wiper fluid. It's cheap. It's

simple. It's easy. And the checkout girl will give you that knowing look, which says, "My God, it's not Valentine's Day. This guy actually has a clue."

Men, let me remind you that Sharon Stone swears that after years of dating and experiencing various yahoos wining and dining her well-toned self, the reason she fell in love with husband Phil Bronstein is simple. When they were first dating, he went camping. On his way out of the woods, clever old Phil picked Sharon a handful of wildflowers and then put them in one of those flimsy paper Dixie cups. When he pulled up to Sharon's house, he put the "bouquet" on his dashboard. . . .

A few months later, they were man and wife, and *The National Enquirer* was predicting it wouldn't last. But it has, partly because Phil is still picking flowers and buying Dixie cups.

If you don't believe it, Drew Barrymore says that the way to her heart isn't diamonds or furs—she loves a man "who will stop in a field and pick me a bunch of wildflowers."

Drew. Sharon. I rest my case.

Think about sending a "Simple-gram." Just scribble a note that says something nice or romantic, for instance: "I love the way you look at me." Copy down song lyrics that move you, or simply write "I love you." People always ask me what the ideal romantic gesture is. You know what I've discovered? There *is* no ideal—it just comes from your heart.

And there's a lot of stress on your heart these days. Much like Valentine's Day, your significant other's birthday also puts a lot of pressure on you, because you feel like you have to do the greatest thing in the world for them, and that isn't heartfelt or sincere. Personally, I'm one of those people who's more likely to give a gift when there isn't an occasion. In other words, I don't like forced fun or romance.

And I don't adhere to a line I once heard, which was: "Romance without finance has no chance." That's ridiculous. Being spontaneous, sexy, and most of all, *there*—heart, mind, body, and soul—is worth more than anything else.

SIMPLE THOUGHT:

"It only takes a minute to get a crush on someone, an hour to like someone, and a day to love someone. But it takes a lifetime to forget them."

— Unknown

obvious things

Here are some things that I've learned to be absolutely (or mostly) true in my almost four decades on this planet.

- Contrary to what my mother said, if you make a horrible face, it will *not* stick that way.

- You really don't need to wait 20 minutes after eating to go swimming—however, I would suggest that you wait that long before going on the stair-stepper.

- Never mix reds with whites in the washing machine, unless you've checked to see if pink is in for summer.

- Unlike what my teacher Mr. Johnson told me, I really didn't need algebra to lead a happy, fulfilled life.

- With all due respect to Europe, no one in the U.S. can really figure out the metric system.

- You *do* have to eat your veggies, but when covered in teriyaki sauce, anything tastes pretty good.

- Boxers or briefs? I say both. Variety is the spice of life. Why get stuck in a rut?

- If a screaming child is carried on to an airplane, chances are she'll be sitting next to you. The same rule applies at theaters or restaurants. But before you give the parents "the look," remember that one day, that child could be your own.

- If you're in the "10 items or less" line at the grocery store, the person in front of you will have 35. And he'll pay with a check. From an account closed two years ago. Oh, and he forgot to present his coupons.

- There's no crying in Tae Bo.

SIMPLE THOUGHT:

"There are two things to aim for in life: first, to get what you want; and, after that, to enjoy it. Only the wisest of mankind achieves the second."

— Logan Pearsall Smith

manic things

We live in a world where it's not easy to be calm, cool, and collected. Who wouldn't be upset when the ketchup bottle crashes down on your big toe just as the broiler starts shooting flames, and then the call comes that your husband isn't even coming home for dinner? The kids are screaming, the field trip form was supposed to be signed two days ago, and the dog is three lawns away, plotting his escape to a new life.

It seems that whenever I'm involved in a scene such as the one above, that's the ideal moment for the phone to ring. I'll dash for it, and of course, it's a telephone solicitor. "No, thank you," I tell them. "I'm not doing a survey about my TV-watching habits, because I don't know Will from Grace, and I think *Dawson's Creek* sounds like a place trying to sell me a time-share."

Excuse me, you've just witnessed one of my manic moments. We all have them. In fact, it's very easy these days to live in panic mode. Every single thing seems to be a major catastrophe. Your daughter has the flu. *Zap!* The creep next to you at work is stealing your ideas. *Kaboom!* The car won't start, and you're going to miss the first five minutes of *Jaws 9: This Time, It's Really Personal. Blammo!*

As you can clearly see, there are real problems and minor anxieties that we turn into major melodramas for no reason at all. To simplify, you really need to evaluate the level of trauma on a scale of one to ten.

Let's say you're trying to emulate Chef

Emeril Lagasse, and in your fervor, you slice and dice your own hand, to the point that the red stuff all over the kitchen isn't tomato sauce. That's true meltdown time in my book. I hate blood. The E.R. should only be visited on Thursday nights—in your sweats while surrounded by snack foods.

The flip side to real disaster is that morning when your alarm doesn't ring, your daughter won't get out of the bathroom, and your dog is ignoring you as if he doesn't understand English. You know he probably speaks several languages—after all, he's a German shepherd. Yes, it's annoying, even troublesome. It might get you in a pinch at work. But it's no real reason to flip out.

I was talking with a friend of mine who couldn't pull her car into the garage of her condo building the other day because someone had blocked the driveway. She slammed out of her vehicle and had a major shouting match with the culprit—only to regret later that she didn't keep her lip zipped while berating the 90-year-old maintenance man. "It was the culmination of a really hard day and I just lost it," she says. "I was so ashamed of myself later."

Realize that stress doesn't happen because the world has made some pact against you personally. Or the Council on All Things Having to Do with Bad Days got together and said, "We know Jim must wake up at five in the morning to do a radio show, so let's make sure the entire cast of *Stomp* is staying in the room right above him, and obviously they must practice only when the moon shines."

I was much more of a "panic person" when I was younger. In college, I drove myself into a frenzy of Pepto-Bismol experiences. I was certainly flunking Spanish and would never graduate—and then I would be broke, penniless, and begging for money on street corners. Of course I'd be the first person in history whose life was ruined because I couldn't figure out how to ask how to use the john in a foreign language. I drove myself nuts worrying about it.

I'm embarrassed to tell you the sheer panic of the situation when I got a flat tire for the first time. It's not like I got it while lost in the middle of nowhere. Monstrous aliens from a Stephen King novel weren't waiting to take me to their planet. (And if I *was* abducted by aliens, God only knows I'd never be able to communicate with them. After all, I couldn't even figure out Spanish!) No, my car broke down on a perfectly safe and friendly street in Cleveland, where some nice person eventually helped me figure out how to use that weird thing in the trunk technically known as a jack.

John Travolta cracks me up with his

Los Angeles-car-breakdown story. He really should have gone a bit bonkers—there he is in the middle of a dangerous intersection with a flat, and people are whizzing by, swearing and yelling at him for stopping traffic. Of course, no one realized that it was John Travolta.

He felt bad. He felt scummy. He felt like a target. He finally ditched the car and walked up this hill to a house, where he knocked on the door. Imagine you're home cooking omelettes and Mr. Staying Alive is on your doorstep. John recalls, "I begged this man to help me fix my car, and he said that he would for a free dance lesson. I was so keyed up that I would have promised him *anything* at that point."

Yes, even big-time movie stars have meltdowns. So what can *you* do about your own manic moments? I tell myself, "It's okay if I have no clue what to do. I will go through a few tough moments—I've gotten through worse moments before in my life. Every tough moment actually does make me stronger and smarter." For instance, I found out that a car jack is for use on your tires. Who knew?

Also, think about times when you've been ready to lose it. Were you really at a total loss, or could you perhaps have said, "Okay, I'm upset (crazed, mad, ready to throw something), but I know what to do"? Knowing what to do will fix just about anything.

But it's also important to know when there's nothing you can do. When a singer drops out of one of my shows on the day of a performance due to a cold, I used to panic. But I realized there was nothing I could do about it, so why waste my energy fretting? Yes, it stinks, and I wish it didn't ever happen. But that's life.

Due to my concert schedule, I'm constantly on airplanes. Imagine that it's the day of a big show and the Midwest is socked in with snow. I drag myself to an airline counter, say a tiny prayer, and hear the words, "Mr. Brickman, your flight has been canceled. We can rebook you tomorrow." Panic mode! But then it dawns on me: *Short of actually sneaking out onto the runway, hijacking a plane, and then taking a quick flight lesson, I can't do anything about it.* I can just call my travel agent and hope for the best.

I remember one time when I had a huge show in Boston, which was in the middle of a blizzard. One flight after another was canceled, and I spent 12 hours at O'Hare Airport in Chicago. There I was, trying to get to Boston on airlines that ranged from United to Air Africa. Finally, I got out and actually made it to the theater exactly five minutes before the curtain went up. The audience never knew how many Bayer Extra Strength Aspirin I had that day. But it worked out.

I can even top that one. Once I was playing at the White House. Yes, it was a true thrill, especially when you realize, *This is actually the real thing and better than that show* The West Wing. But the deal was that anyone playing this gala benefit for President Clinton had to attend a special rehearsal on a specific afternoon. Unfortunately, on the evening that the rehearsal was to take place, I had a show in Philly. But if you didn't make the rehearsal, you weren't in the White House show.

I took a deep breath, cursed, checked the dates 32 times, cursed some more, and then realized that my mantra would come in handy: *Okay, I know what to do*. What to do was simple. Sort of.

My tour manager had a car waiting outside the White House, and we started driving to Philly the minute rehearsals were over at 1600 Pennsylvania Avenue—no stopping at the Golden Arches, no bathroom breaks. In fact, there were no liquids in that car at all—it was just driving and checking the clock. About 400 times. Oh, there were also a few choice words said to that minivan in front of us going 20 miles under the speed limit.

I made it within a few minutes of the show. Poor Anne Cochran was in the theater running an iron over my clothes and planning to stall if I was late.

In the end, it worked out, but with a few regrets—I let my panic stop me from enjoying my first trip to the White House. Worry wrecks enjoyment. Think about how many times you've missed the fun part of something because of needless anxiety. It's almost criminal to rob yourself in this manner.

Just realize that things *will* go wrong. Freaking out isn't going to make it better.

SIMPLE
THOUGHT:

"When you get to the end of your rope, tie a knot and hang on."

— Franklin D. Roosevelt

beautiful things

I'm writing this standing at my kitchen sink, eating tuna out of the can. I wish I could tell you that it's my snack of choice in the wee hours of the morning, but honestly, I hate each salty bite.

The tuna is part of my new high-protein diet. My brain screams out for macaroni and cheese. I eat a slice of fat-free (and tasteless) turkey—my body dreams of bagels slathered in cream cheese and jelly. My lips have to pretend that this gray fish is better than homemade apple pie covered in cinnamon ice cream.

I better stop now. I'll probably gain

weight just from mentally digesting these dream foods. But it's time to face facts: I'm getting older, and my waistline is getting wider. As for my metabolism, it's getting . . . what? Time off for good behavior? Vacation? It just sort of goes AWOL from time to time. And that's tough for me to accept. You see, my idea of a proper Queen isn't Elizabeth, but Dairy. But now I have to cool it, and I actually want to lose a few pounds—hence, the protein mania.

And it's hell. Or as Bette Davis said, "Growing old ain't for sissies"—and she never really got to enjoy this age of nips, tucks, eye jobs, various implants, and Hollywood jobs that require everyone to look like they're dewy-eyed 25-year-olds. The "dewy" part out here usually comes with a plastic surgeon, and a bill not covered by most major insurance companies.

Growing older isn't simple anymore—

for anyone. It's even rougher when you're in the public eye. For instance, yesterday my record company calls and says, "Jim, you're not getting any younger. Something must be done about your hair."

They've actually had a meeting about my hair. Imagine 12 people in various designer suits sitting around a mahogany conference table in New York City, sipping coffee and eating doughnuts or fat-free muffins. One says, "Okay, let's get to the big stuff. Should Brickman color his hair, or should he leave it grayish? Are we selling that he's almost 40?"

You think Sting and Bruce Springsteen are immune from these types of discussions? No way.

My record company gurus went on to ask each other big questions about my new grown-up look, such as: "Should we put him into that Ralph Lauren woodsy category?

Does Jim look good in corduroy?"

If you're only 20, skip this chapter. If you're my age, it's fine to admit that you're balding on top. It's weird for me to tell you that this morning I did something really strange, something I would have never done if I wasn't in the public eye. Yes, I caved in—I colored my hair. Now I have the following questions: *Is this going to make me a better piano player? Am I suddenly way more handsome? Do I look 20 again?* And most important: *Do I care?*

Face it. We're never happy with how we look. I know so many women who for years have struggled to copy the "Rachel" haircut—the one Jennifer Aniston famously wore several years ago on *Friends*. I know that as a guy, it's really not my business to say, "But Betty Sue, you have naturally curly hair, which really doesn't lend itself to the 'Rachel.'" Those are the types of comments that get guys in trouble, so I just keep my mouth shut.

But I can't keep my mouth shut any longer. I live in Los Angeles and I know some stuff. For instance, can you just trust me on this—the reason Jennifer Aniston has that glorious hair is that there's this pressure on her to look perfect—and she's surrounded by 12 stylists who blow, flatten, straighten, flip, flop, gel, mousse, spray, laminate, and shellac it into place. It's not simple. It's not attainable for any of the rest of us. *Give it up.*

Which is easy for me to say as I stuff myself with protein to lose weight—which I don't recommend to anyone, because I'm not a diet guy. I don't even know if this is working. All I know is that I would kill someone for a piece of Wonder Bread. But you get the picture—I want to look like I'm 30. You want to look like Gwyneth Paltrow. It's all the same thing.

Why can't we just look like ourselves? Why can't we create a personal style and not adopt one sanctioned by some magazine or TV show?

I can even tell you a rather pathetic story about my style. You see, there's this pair of pants that I love to wear on stage. My friend Anne will say, "Jim, can you burn those ugly pants? They're really ratty looking." So just to keep everyone happy, I tell a tiny white lie and say, "Oh, this is the last weekend for them."

And then something startling happened. No, the pants did not disintegrate on stage, thus causing me to be arrested for indecent exposure. But hey, that would be a good story to tell the kids someday.

What happened was this: One morning I'm sifting through the feedback cards from audience members, and I read, "I love your pants. Where did you get them?" (Memo to

Anne: I have the card. I can show it to you. Just call me.)

The point is that I'm happy that my pants finally have the recognition they deserve. But I'm scared, too. Now, I'm Jennifer Aniston—I'm setting a fashion trend. Will ratty-looking pants start sweeping the nation? Will Anne have to move to a foreign country just to see men dressed in linen that still creases? Will Brad Pitt someday have to color his hair? Does he do it already?

The mind boggles.

The point isn't that beauty comes from within. Ugh. We all know that beauty comes from Maybelline and Estée Lauder. And I can live with that . . . within reason. I just wish we would stop putting this pressure on ourselves to live up to an ideal set by Hollywood.

Why not come up with your own

style—but please, for my sake, skip the blue eye shadow. Let your hair go gray. Wear that plaid shirt that says "Bubba's Moose Lodge." Remember when Sharon Stone wore a Gap T-shirt to the Oscars and everyone said, "Oh, yeah! I love those shirts"? Of course, everyone subsequently started wearing Gap T-shirts to everything from proms to weddings.

The simplest advice here is to just do what makes you feel comfortable. Me? I'm wearing those ratty pants to every city in the United States.

SIMPLE THOUGHT:

"There are only two things a child will share willingly—communicable diseases and his mother's age."

— Benjamin Spock

the guilt thing

A friend of mine, when pushed to the brink, has a snappy phrase she likes to use: "What don't you understand about *no?* The 'n' or the 'o'?" she quips.

Cute, huh?

But we digress. Here's what I don't understand about that little word. Does saying no to anyone make me the worst person on the face of this earth? Does it make me selfish? Or mean? Or nasty? Or stuck-up? Or the male version of Cruella de Vil mixed with the Wicked Witch?

Let's say the neighbors call and ask me to walk their dog. I really don't want to do it, but I put on my best cheerful (and fake) voice and say, "Of course I'll walk your 190-pound Doberman while you're out for lunch. I'm sure Killer and I will get along great. Don't worry about my wounds from the last time. Doc says the stitches will come out any day now."

A lot of us put ourselves in these types of situations. For instance, a friend of mine repeatedly gets stuck driving her neighborhood's car pool, which she doesn't mind that much, except on days when she needs a break. But can she say the "n" or the "o"?

Now say it with me: *"No."*

Ooooh, it felt good. But "No, thank you" will also do.

Like you, I'm a card-carrying "yes man." Take the other night, for example. I'm writing my new album in Nashville and—I probably shouldn't tell you this—I usually don't register in hotels under an alias. So,

I'm at a Hyatt under something sneaky like "J. Brickman"—how crafty of me—and at one in the morning, the phone rings. I grope around for the receiver and finally whisper, "Hellooooo." I hear a voice on the other end saying, "Hey, Jimbo, I'm just wondering what time you're going on tomorrow for this charity benefit?"

I honestly thought it was the sound guy. But it was just someone named Steve going, "I'm a really big fan of yours, and I'm sorry to call you in the middle of the night, but I just wanted to say hello and find out when your show starts." My brain is screaming, "No, no, no. I'm sleeping, Steve-o." But the nice guy inside that would make Miss Manners proud says, "Hi, Steve. Thanks for calling. I'll be on at 11 A.M. Hope to see ya there."

It's tricky with fans. You wonder about stuff, such as: Is this just a nice normal fan who wants to meet me—which is really cool—or is it someone who might know that I'm staying in the hotel and they're lurking outside room 1302? Is he gonna beat me up because I wrote a love song that was his and his girlfriend's make-out song until she jilted him?

Mostly, I do want to meet people. I want to shake everyone's hand, and I want them to think of me as a nice guy—which is what all of us want in this life. And that's what makes it so hard to go with your true feelings—it means that you're not able to be all things to all people.

It's tough. I get e-mails from people asking me to play at their weddings. We try to respond to everything, but sometimes a letter will slip through the cracks. Once that happened and I got a nasty e-mail back: "Dear Jim, I thought you were a nice guy, but you ignored my wedding request." I felt bad about this for weeks; I felt guilty. But then I realized that you can't possibly please everyone. There are times when you have to say no to your friends, your boss, or even your family. You have to say no to your children—no matter what the consequences.

A friend of mine told her three-year-old son that he couldn't have Taco Bell for dinner one night. The little boy ran out into the middle of the driveway and started screaming at the top of his lungs: *"Help! Help! Help!"* Can you even imagine? The neighbors came racing over to save the kid's life, and they saw a sobbing little Tyler standing there with his whole body shaking. He wailed, "I want t-t-t-tacos! But Mommy said no!" Once everyone realized nothing serious was going on, the other moms broke into laughter.

"God, it would have been so much easier to cave in," one mom said to my friend.

"We're really proud of you for standing your ground."

Sometimes, you just have to say no. No to a crazed fan who calls in the middle of the night. No to your mother. No to Millie and Herbert who want me to play "Valentine" when they walk down the aisle. Believe me, I would love to play at everyone's wedding, but the simple fact is that we all have to draw the line somewhere and make choices.

Just like you, I wish I could say yes to everyone. I really, really do.

SIMPLE THOUGHT:

"To err is human,
but it feels divine."

— Mae West

healthy things

I believe in naps, but it wasn't always that way. Just ask my mother:

"James never required sleep. When he was two years old, I'd say to him, 'Baby Mike is taking his nap, and Mommy's taking her nap.' And James would say to me, 'Who's taking my nap?' He refused to sleep."

Was I nuts? Now I love to catnap, and lately I've heard great news about my little afternoon habit. First of all, I was thrilled to read a nationwide survey from the National Sleep Foundation that said Americans don't get enough sleep. Hear! Hear!—I love this foundation. For every single person who has ever tried to wake up a groggy Jim in the afternoon, well, that survey will be mailed to you shortly. But frankly, no one needed to spend the money for that study— they could have just asked me, or any new mother or father.

I'm certainly not a medical professional, and I don't even watch *ER* with any regularity, but I also read something else recently that's a simple way to improve your health: Get out in the sun. Apparently, sunlight stimulates the body's natural immune system. As little as 20 minutes a day will rev you up. Of course, protect yourself from too much sun—ask your doctor about that part.

Now for the really good health news. Are you ready? Imagine my joy when I read that some German scientists are claiming that laziness is "the antidote to professional stress." In other words, people who spend an afternoon swaying in a hammock instead of training for a 10K race are not only better rested, but they'll live longer, too. Professor Peter Axt, the author of this glorious study—called "The Joy of Laziness"—suggests that we actually should spend half of our free time *just doing nothing. Nada! Zero!* This is my kind of science guy.

Oh, here's my last moment of playing doctor. Skip espresso if you need a jolt—a regular old cup of coffee actually has more caffeine.

Thank you. My bill will be in the mail.

SIMPLE THOUGHT:

"Happiness is good health and a bad memory."

— Ingrid Bergman

risky things

When I first thought of recording my solo piano music, it was really for myself. I hadn't planned on taking it to record companies. I did it to express myself, and to let out some feelings I had inside.

Back then, it had been a long time since I'd just played the piano. I would use it for my work in advertising, but I'd never really played for my heart or my soul. After I'd finished my six-song demo, my friends and family told me that they thought it was good enough to buy and I should do something with it. That's when it all changed for me, creatively. I took a chance.

It's so hard these days to allow yourself

to take a leap of faith. But scary can become thrilling. Risk can turn into reward.

Did I tell you the story of when I decided to move to L.A.? I was 28 years old and had spent my whole life living in Cleveland. I was secure. My friends and family were close by, and I had a cool dry cleaner— what more does a guy want in life? But there was this nagging feeling in my gut that there *was* more for me . . . just not in Cleveland. So I pretty much packed up and moved to L.A. in one day. It was one of those nutty moves where something snaps and you *become* the Nike ad: Just do it, Jim.

It sounds so glamorous, but the truth is, I didn't have any money, and I didn't know one person in L.A. I moved into this run-down apartment complex filled with the young and the extremely restless. At age 28, you don't want your neighbors having keg parties. Plus, there was the whole Southern California culture in my face—I had a stomach; they had abs. Buff didn't mean something you did to your car.

I think that for about a year, I walked around in a complete daze. I wasn't even sure what the hell I was doing there, and I was homesick like crazy. I became a Sunday night CBS movie because everything was just so dramatic—sometimes I'd moan out loud, "I wonder what will happen to me?" Believe me, next to that Oliver kid who begged for more food, I was the most pathetic creature on the planet.

It wasn't simple at all. I wasn't prepared for the L.A. lifestyle. You call a doctor and hear, "He's not here. He's driving his daughter to ballet class." I learned from L.A. that your life is equally as important as what you do—and it doesn't hurt to announce it. I learned how to say, "I can't meet with you today because I'm flossing my teeth." But all kidding aside, the more I opened up to my new life, the more it opened up to me.

I took a risk. I did something completely foreign. And, as with any chance, it was scary. But I can give you a few tips. First, if you move to a new place, the best thing to do is work on creating your world within your new spot. Find the local dry cleaner, the best deli for corned beef sandwiches on rye, and the best route to the post office. It's your way of seizing some control over your new frontier. Suddenly, the only risks to me in L.A. were the earthquakes and being mugged by those kids who have 27 earrings. But what's life without a few risks?

SIMPLE THOUGHT:

*"If you risk nothing,
then you risk everything."*

— Geena Davis

miraculous things

Sometimes we feel as if the only way to communicate is through words, but I feel that my music also says something to people. I truly believe that it's the way I speak. Maybe it's another language.

My ability to speak without words was never more clear than when I met Brittany, an autistic little girl with a passion and a gift for music. Her mother introduced her to me before a concert in Columbia, South Carolina. Suddenly, this beautiful little girl was on stage, sitting at my piano, and her mom whispered, "Honey, this is Mr. Brickman. He's the man who writes all the beautiful music that you like to play."

Suddenly, this big smile spread across her tiny face, and her hands touched the keyboards. She began playing, as if by magic, a song of mine called "Angel Eyes." She played it to perfection. And what was even more uncanny was that she also performed with all the emotion that I had infused into the piece. It was like she connected completely with the notes, but also with the feelings and heartfelt power of the music.

For the longest time, she sat at my piano bench not speaking a word. I finally asked her if she'd play a duet of "Valentine" with me. Gingerly, I put my hands on the piano keys. She smiled in a shy, wondrous way, and carefully placed her hands on the keys, too . . . and then we took off on a duet that was thrilling.

Ordinary miracles are all around us.

They're humbling in their simplicity.

I remember a few years ago, my grand-mother Gert called me and asked if I could come play the piano for her friends in her nursing home in Chicago. She'd told all her cronies about her grandson James, the crazy musician. Her fondest wish was that I could perform for them. To be honest, I was in Chicago for one day for a concert. I had a jam-packed schedule of radio-station appearances and interviews. Everyone was advising me to do the nursing-home show another time. We'd get to it later.

But something in my gut told me I *had* to do it. I arrived without Anne Cochran, my singer, who was busy. And from the start, it was a little rocky. During my first song, an 85-year-old woman yelled out, "Where's the girl who sings for you?!" Heckled by a sen-ior citizen! But my grandmother just laughed. In fact, she was beaming with

pride. James was her boy, and he was playing for her friends.

Two days later, my grandmother died.

The point is that you have to look at the
world with awe. You can't be so busy that
you don't open your ears and hear what
other people need to make their own magic.
And you have to appreciate magic enough
to be ready for miracles—such as an autistic
girl who wants to do a duet.

SIMPLE THOUGHT:

*"Whether you think that
you can, or that you can't,
you are usually right."*

— Henry Ford

change things

In the end, it's up to you to get off the treadmill. It's up to you to leave the phone unplugged and ignore the e-mails. You *can* lose your cell phone . . . and in the process, you might find your life again.

You can remember the joys of hide-and-seek at dusk, Mother-May-I, and running through a sprinkler on a blazing hot summer morning. You can still eat Red Hots until your tongue burns, and figure out who the villain is on a *Scooby-Doo* cartoon. You can remember the joy of bedtime prayers and goodnight kisses. We know you can hail a taxi—you can also *still* flag down the Good

Humor man, even if it means running half a block with your spare change warm in your hand, screaming, "Stop! Please! Stop!"

When's the last time you ran until you were out of breath—or laughed so hard that you actually doubled over? When's the last time you remembered your first kiss—or ate a Popsicle with the orange liquid running down your fingers, or called your best friend and double-dog-dared him to get on a plane and visit? Wouldn't a good game of dodgeball solve most of the world's problems?

Louisa May Alcott, author of *Little Women,* didn't have any of the modern temptations. She wasn't pressured to buy the latest workout tape or CD-ROM—she didn't even count carbs. And that's good for the rest of us, because she could put everything into perspective: *"Far away there in the sunshine are my highest aspirations. I may not reach them, but I can look up and see their beauty, believe in them, and try to follow where they lead."*

It's simple advice.

SIMPLE THOUGHT:

"If you can dream it, you can do it."

— Walt Disney

about
jim brickman

Jim Brickman is one of America's hottest new pop stars. His dazzling piano artistry and clever songwriting skills have led to sales of more than three million albums. Hits such as "Valentine" and "The Gift" have helped build his reputation as America's most romantic songwriter. In theaters across the country, Brickman turns a simple concert stage into an intimate space where imagination takes off, using musical notes to weave a tapestry of emotion, color, and spirit.

Jim's Website is:
www.JimBrickman.com

about
cindy pearlman

Cindy Pearlman is a nationally syndicated entertainment writer for the *New York Times Syndicate* and the *Chicago Sun-Times*. Her work has appeared in *Entertainment Weekly, Premiere, People, Ladies' Home Journal, McCall's, Seventeen, Movieline,* and *Cinescape*. Over the past 15 years, she has interviewed Hollywood's biggest stars, who appear in her column "The Big Picture."

HAY HOUSE
LIFESTYLES TITLES
OF RELATED INTEREST

<u>Flip Books</u>

101 Ways to Happiness, by Louise L. Hay
101 Ways to Romance,
    by Barbara De Angelis, Ph.D.
101 Ways to Transform Your Life,
    by Dr. Wayne W. Dyer

<u>Books</u>

A Garden of Thoughts, by Louise L. Hay
Dream Journal, by Leon Nacson
Inner Wisdom, by Louise L. Hay
Meditations, by Sylvia Browne
Prayers, by Sylvia Browne
    (available February 2002)
You Can Heal Your Life Gift Edition,
    by Louise L. Hay
You Can Heal Your Life Companion Book,
    by Louise L. Hay (available January 2002)

Card Decks

The Four Agreements Cards,
    by DON Miguel Ruiz
Inner Peace Cards, by Dr. Wayne W. Dyer
Power Thought Cards, by Louise L. Hay
Wisdom Cards, by Louise L. Hay
Zen Cards, by Daniel Levin

All of the above titles may be ordered
by calling Hay House at the
numbers on the following page.

We hope you enjoyed this Hay House Lifestyles book. If you would like to receive a free catalog featuring additional Hay House books and products, or if you would like information about the Hay Foundation, please contact:

Hay House, Inc.
P.O. Box 5100
Carlsbad, CA 92018-5100

(760) 431-7695 or **(800) 654-5126**
(760) 431-6948 (fax) or
(800) 650-5115 (fax)

Please visit the Hay House Website at:
hayhouse.com